A BEGINNER'S GUIDE TO JAPAN

A BEGINNER'S GUIDE TO JAPAN

Observations and Provocations

PICO IYER

ALFRED A. KNOPF · NEW YORK · 2019

THIS IS A BORZOI BOOK PUBLISHED BY ALFRED A. KNOPF

Copyright © 2019 by Pico Iyer

All rights reserved. Published in the United States by Alfred A. Knopf, a division of Penguin Random House LLC, New York, and in Canada by Random House of Canada, a division of Penguin Random House Canada Limited, Toronto.

www.aaknopf.com

Knopf, Borzoi Books, and the colophon are registered trademarks of Penguin Random House LLC.

Library of Congress Cataloging-in-Publication Data
Names: Iyer, Pico, author.
Title: A beginner's guide to Japan : observations and provocations by Pico Iyer.
Description: First edition. | New York : Alfred A. Knopf, 2019.
Identifiers: LCCN 2018038539 (print) | LCCN 2018039527 (ebook) | ISBN 9780451493965 (ebook) | ISBN 9780451493958 (hardcover) | ISBN 9781524711733 (open market)
Subjects: LCSH: Iyer, Pico—Travel—Japan. | Japan—Description and travel.
Classification: LCC DS811 (ebook) | LCC DS811 .I95 2019 (print) | DDC 952.05—dc23
LC record available at https://lccn.loc.gov/2018038539

Jacket design by Abby Weintraub

Manufactured in the United States of America
First Edition

From crazy title to eccentric procedure, this little book owes almost everything to wildly generous Annie Dillard, champion of things seen and unseen, with a heart the size of Forbes Field; and to Robert Richardson, model of selflessness and grace, beautifully elevating writer and gentleman.

Thank you both.

Attention, taken to its highest degree, is the same thing as prayer.

—SIMONE WEIL

CONTENTS

A BEGINNER'S GUIDE TO JAPAN

I've been living in western Japan for more than thirty-two years, and, to my delight, I know far less than when I arrived. A land of streamlined surfaces gives you very much what you expect—and so much you didn't expect, under the surface, that you don't know what to do with it. The home of collected inwardness has also shown me daily how much, as Proust observed, "a change in the weather is sufficient to recreate the world, and ourselves."

I've never studied Japan or worked here, and I stay in Nara on a tourist visa to remind myself how out-of-it I remain. I speak the language as a two-year-old girl might, since such Japanese as I know I've picked up from my wife, and in Japan even the word for "I" is different for a woman and a man. But I've been with my Kyoto-born wife—and our entirely Japanese kids—for more than thirty-two years now, most of them in an anonymous suburb where no other foreigners are to be seen. I seldom speak English in Japan, and in any case Japan has taught me how deeply the truest things lie beyond the reach of any language.

Much of this book may infuriate anyone who knows Japan; it infuriates me most of the time. Assertions in one section seem to contradict those in another, and what appears to belong in the temple appears in a section on the love-hotel, and vice versa. A lot of what I ascribe to Japan clearly applies to much of East Asia, and some of what I see in Kyoto you'd never find in more rural areas.

No matter. These are simply provocations, opening lines designed to quicken you to better comebacks of your own. "The opposite of a great truth," as they say in the temples of Kyoto, "is also true." I've tried to order my salvos so you travel, as most of us do, from the noisy, congested streets to impeccably well-made-up interiors to, at last, that private domain where you can't even think in terms of "Japan" or "the West." But if you read out of sequence in this fan-shaped book, now on a jam-packed train, now in a noiseless temple, you'll be taking in the country as most of us do, bumping from the strange to the familiar and back again.

I call this a "beginner's guide" not only because it's aimed at beginners, but mostly because it's written by one. Being in Japan has taught me to say, "I wonder," more often than "I think." The first rule for any foreigner in Japan is not to talk of this-or-that; the second is never to take anything too seriously.

ON THE STREETS

THE ENIGMAS OF ARRIVAL

There are eleven arrows on the sign above you, as you disembark in Kyoto Station. They point left, right, straight ahead and backwards. In the middle is a question mark.

•

Platform 0 is close to Platforms 31 and 32, and a large "Restaurant Guide" board informs you that there are one hundred and seven dining options around the station alone. There are also twenty-two hotels in the immediate vicinity, just one of which offers fifteen banquet halls, five hundred and sixteen rooms, a halal menu, a clinic, a photo salon and a church.

•

So much is available, almost nothing can be found. You're in a living Web site of sorts—boxes and links popping up on every side, leading to art gallery and "Happy Terrace," to six-story post office and thirteen-floor department store—but nobody's given you the password.

•

There are snatches of English, French, German everywhere, but serving almost as decoration—like colors or sounds—and surrounded by characters in three non-overlapping alphabets. The net effect is of a hundred and one people speaking a thousand and two languages, none of which they understand.

•

There are no addresses, it's said, in Japan—or, worse, there are collections of numbers, but sometimes they refer to the chronology of construction, sometimes to something else. When my daughter, my wife, and I write down the address of the flat we've all shared, each one of us inscribes a completely different street name.

•

Before the West arrived, there were twice as many T-junctions and dead ends in Tokyo as there were thoroughfares. A castle town needs to confound invaders. After World War II, the city was reconstructed along the pathways that had come up around the rubble of bombed buildings, rendering the terrain even more impenetrable.

•

On the train into Kyoto, I point out to my Japanese wife a sweet ad full of teddy bears, one sporting a badge, another next to a bright-red ambulance.

"Yes," she says. "It says that if you see a child who's been beaten, please call that number. If you do not, the child may die!"

"And that picture of the cute fox and bear exchanging whispers?"

"A lawyer," says Hiroko. "If you have some kind of accident, he can help."

DRESSING THE PART

After a rabbit appeared in Japan in 1873, the craze for the creatures grew so intense that a single animal fetched the equivalent of twenty thousand dollars.

·

After a woman threw herself off the roof of a Tokyo apartment complex in 1970, roughly one hundred and fifty others threw themselves off the same roof.

·

I board the train on a Saturday morning, and face a gaggle of schoolkids in uniform, lines of businessmen with badges on their lapels, squadrons of young women in dark suits. The next day I board the same train, to be greeted by a young guy in sockless canvas shoes and his date clomping along in high-fashion snowshoes (in a place where snow is all but unknown). Everyone's taken on a part, but in the off-hours, even partners may find they're acting in different plays.

·

Thus, Japanese couples on honeymoon traditionally plan matching outfits for every hour of their trip. Even girls on a Sunday shopping spree often sport the same hairstyles, false eyelashes and white boots. Fashion becomes less about standing out than fitting in, at least within the micro-group of which you are a part.

•

For a foreigner, therefore, clothes don't make the man here; they simply mark the role. But roles shift at the speed of light in Japan, as people adopt a radically different voice (even a different word for "I") for colleague and secretary and boss. If it's treacherous to judge a book by its cover, how much more so if it's a foreign book and has a dozen covers to go with every audience.

•

In 1999, I sought out the man said to have invented karaoke, to tell him that my editors at *Time* had chosen him as one of the "100 Asians of the Century." He handed me in response a business card advertising his services as a dog trainer.

•

That mild-mannered matron with her hands in her lap, dressed as for church, is, my wife explains to me, a wild thing, ready to do anything with anyone. And that rail-thin twenty-three-year-old model in fishnet stockings, perfectly made up, turns out, her startled Californian boyfriend tells me, never to have had a boyfriend before.

●

Whenever we're abroad, I have to spend hours persuading my wife to dress down, since dressing up will make everybody around us feel underdressed. For her, putting on a designer outfit to go to the ATM is as much a sign of courtesy as wearing black to a funeral or speaking in complete sentences.

●

Two out of every five Japanese men pluck their eyebrows—and the first geisha, in the thirteenth century, were men. "It is best that you carry powdered rouge in your sleeve pocket," an eighteenth-century manual for samurai advises. "We sometimes are of bad color when sobering up, lying down or rising."

●

My wife said she'd never seen a real man in Japan, an American friend who grew up in Tokyo tells me—until she met a Kabuki actor who specialized in taking the part of women.

•

No one but the simpleminded would call my neighbors "two-faced"; they command a huge repertoire of faces, to deal with every setting, and we who describe that phenomenon in entirely different terms to lover and to mother can only conclude that we're much the same, but with a narrower range.

•

The Buddha himself took pains to say opposite things in different situations, since what works for a crowd of monks will make no sense to a group of businessmen. What we call "inconsistency" speaks in fact for a consistent wish to do the appropriate thing.

EMPIRE OF SMILES

irls in Japan are trained to put the right earring on with the left hand, because it looks more attractive.

•

Young women in Japan are also trained to seem as cheerful, as sweet—as girlish—as teenagers. Since we often try to seem sophisticated, we don't always know what to do with those who aspire to seem innocent and wide-eyed.

•

A celebrated French semiotician wrote a ludicrous book on Japan called *Empire of Signs;* what he failed to see was that Japan is in truth an Empire of Smiles, smiles being more human, more alluring and much more emotionally complex than any sign.

•

"Jaguar model names sound like rockets," notes Paul Beatty in *The Sellout.* "XJ-S, XJ8, E-Type. Hondas sound like cars designed by pacifists and humanitarian diplomats. The Accord, Civic, Insight."

Japan believes in accentuating the positive—black markets after the war were known as "blue-sky markets," a Tokyo garbage fill was called "Dream Island"—because it knows that the Buddha's First Noble Truth posits the reality of suffering. When a character in a Yasujiro Ozu movie smiles, it says more about sadness than any sob or spasm might.

·

"You Europeans think it disgraceful to expose your bodies," a Japanese host explained to a visiting writer in the 1920s, "but you shamelessly expose your minds. Everyone knows how men and women are made, so we have no shame in uncovering our bodies. We think it improper to uncover our thoughts."

·

If nothing's personal in public Japan, you may conclude that Japan is an impersonal place. But as the woman in the tiny patisserie flashes you a beautiful smile and spends many long minutes placing your $1.50 éclair in a pink box, enclosing a bag of ice so the pastry won't melt on the long way home, wrapping the box in seasonal paper and appending a bow (pick any color) under a badge to keep the box shut, you're really in the realm of the transpersonal. Everything is deeply personal; it just has nothing to do with you.

•

Even in love, living with a longtime Japanese boyfriend, the British novelist Angela Carter "used to turn over in my mind from time to time the question: how far does a pretense of feeling, maintained with absolute conviction, become authentic?"

•

The British, after all, tend to wink at the part they're assigned in the national pantomime; in pre-ironic Japan, it's much more important to be earnest. Style is less the enemy of sincerity, as Oscar Wilde had it, than its public expression.

•

My friends in Japan are more expert at posing for photographs, at singing on cue, even at stepping onstage than nearly anyone I know in the West.

But ask them what they think or feel, and they look uneasy and say nothing.

●

The Japanese artist Takashi Murakami has won a storm of global recognition by titling his exhibitions *Ego,* by setting up shops in the middle of his shows, by receiving thirteen million dollars for a single piece even though the pieces no longer issue from his hand.

When I spent a whole day with Murakami to conduct a public conversation with him in Los Angeles, however—he came onstage dressed as a cartoon clown—I saw what a thoughtful and precise, deeply Japanese soul he is, even while playing the opposite. He grew quiet, almost reverent, when I spoke of the anime director Hayao Miyazaki, whom he called his "guru and mentor"; it was his doctorate in classical Japanese painting, I realized, that schooled Murakami-san in the traditions that now he was turning upside down.

The *serufu-esutimu* he broadcasts—as with the novelist Natsume Soseki's claim, a hundred years earlier, "Self-centeredness became for me a new beginning"—was simply, I realized, his way of reminding his country not to believe in the shy and self-deprecating role it has taken up on the global stage.

•

A traditional home in Japan—a classical self—is all shifting panels and self-contained compartments. Even as the absence of locks and curtains keeps the individual aware at every moment that she's part of a larger whole.

•

Thus a shoji screen turns a figure into a silhouette, an Ozu movie gives us archetypal characters—Daughter, Father, Neighbor—who move like a commedia dell'arte troupe from film to film. My wife didn't tell me, for years, the name of her boss; calling that boss "Department Head" took the sting out of interactions as calling her "Nakata" never could.

•

This means, in turn, that the theme of most Japanese scenes is less the individual drama than the larger canvas (of Nature, of Time, of gods) against which it plays out. Look at a Hiroshige woodcut—read a haiku—and what you see is not so much a human being as the passage of time, the falling snow, a sense of loneliness.

By making individual figures indistinct—it's the secret of many a Kazuo Ishiguro novel, as of Oscar Wilde fairy tales—one turns a "he" or "she" into a "we."

•

Young societies are distrustful of artifice; older ones—and few are more seasoned than Japan—know that artifice may be all we have in a world where pain is never distant.

THE PERFECT ACTRESS

One foggy night in early March, Hiroko and I went up to Tokyo, at the invitation of an old friend, for the Japanese premiere of *The Iron Lady,* the 2011 film starring Meryl Streep as Margaret Thatcher. It's not the kind of event we're used to attending, living in a forgotten suburb, and as we took our places in the center of one row, brushing past former Japanese prime ministers and their wives, I could hear one or two grumble about the disheveled Indian and his youthful-looking Japanese companion. Most of them were here to enjoy the sensation of meeting onscreen a British leader they'd worked with in life.

Before the film began, Ms. Streep came out to offer a few words of introduction. She was preternaturally gracious and charming and poised. But it was something else that shocked both Hiroko and me. Ten days earlier, we'd seen her accept the Academy Award on TV in a not entirely flattering gold costume that contrived to make her look like a matriarch, a kind of fairy godmother to all the younger beauties seated before her. Now, not three hundred hours on, we found ourselves looking at the most ravishing young beauty we could remember seeing, tall and slender, in little black dress, golden hair tumbling down her back.

We'd guessed she'd been dressing down at the Oscars; the first thing she'd said after collecting her award was "I had this feeling I could hear half of America going, 'Oh no! Oh come on, why? Her—again?'" Besides, she'd been wearing a similarly broad gold dress the last time she'd received an Academy Award, twenty-nine years before. But of all the things for which Meryl Streep is famous—her intellect, her accents, her stamina, her political courage and the makeup artist who, for thirty-seven years at that point, had been turning her into perfect renditions of Karen Silkwood and Isak Dinesen—we'd never heard her drop-dead beauty mentioned.

After the closing credits, our friend invited us to join the star and the director and another friend for an intimate dinner high atop the hotel where they were staying. Through the three hours that followed, Hiroko and I were witness to everything we might have hoped for from the world's most accomplished actress, and much more: she was sparkling, responsive, vulnerable, even haunting. She seemed to shrug off her celebrity, speaking to us as openly, it felt, and as warmly as she did her friends. But when she got up and strode across the empty restaurant at evening's end, far taller than even the waiters, we were reminded that we were forty-five stories above the ground.

On the long trip home, I tried to work out what we'd just seen. I remembered that Streep had told an interviewer that she was drawn to playing Thatcher because the British prime minister seemed so "designed," not the first word that comes to every mind.

I recalled her adding that she felt terrified only when called upon to play Meryl Streep. As a girl, she'd recounted—she'd grown famous for talking about the way women are pushed into boxes—she'd seen that the way to get ahead was by saying as little as possible and just exclaiming, "Wow!" and "Great!" and "Cool!"

In some curious way, I felt that spending an evening with her had opened up to me the society all around. The mystery of Meryl Streep is that we know it's hardly possible, even with a brilliant makeup artist, to be the golden songstress of *Mamma Mia!* one year and the Alzheimer's-stricken prime minister of Britain three years on, to not just resemble—but become— Emmeline Pankhurst and a ragged, leather-jacketed rock star in the same year. The deeper mystery is that, the more she showed herself to us, across the table, the less we could say who she really was.

"You must be happy to be going home after a month on the road," I offered as we stood by the elevator doors, waiting for her to fly away.

She looked startled in the quiet space high above the fog. "I really feel at home," said the perfect actress, "when I work."

MAKING ONESELF UP

Makeup is essential to a society in which public face is crucial—and in which making up with everyone is an indispensable part of sustaining a larger harmony.

•

"My colleague spends two hours a day making herself up," my wife says, on her way to the department store where she works.

"She wants everyone to look at her?"

"No. She wants everyone not to."

•

Hiroko will spend twenty minutes hastily applying makeup just to go to the grocery store around the corner. But when even the most elegant visitor comes to our flat, she thinks nothing of running around with no makeup, in T-shirt and jeans.

•

The Japanese, famously, have separate words for the self inside the home and the one that's out on the streets. But what is less often noticed is that many spaces are a kind of transit zone, effectively public sites turned into private thoroughfares.

●

"Everybody wants to look their best," advises the notice in a Brooklyn subway car, filthy with trash and smeared with graffiti, "but it's a subway car not a restroom." In Japan, however, the subway car really is a public convenience that serves (since everyone contrives not to look at everyone else) as a private antechamber.

●

The New York subway, however quixotically, bans "Clipping" and "Primping," though everything else seems more than permitted. In Japan, where carriages are spotless and people highly proper, every other woman seems to be applying final touches to lips and eyes and cheeks as the train pulls into her station.

●

The Japanese are as adept at not looking as they are at not speaking. In Bunraku drama, the three black-clad puppet masters are seated onstage; yet the audience silently consents to see only the dolls that the masters are manipulating.

•

Strangers routinely sleep with their heads on strangers' shoulders on Japanese trains, and the leaned-upon agree not to flinch. A sign of trust— of community, perhaps—but also a reminder that what constitutes public and what constitutes private is something subtler than homes and walls.

•

To make oneself up, in a deeper way, is a mark of courtesy. In the face of great suffering, the very English novelist Jane Gardam writes, an English person has to put on a brave face, "a mask slapped on out of consideration, out of a wish not to increase concern and also out of a genetic belief that our feelings are diminished when we show them."

•

When Ansel Adams took pictures of Japanese internees in Californian concentration camps during World War II, his subjects were so determined to offer bright smiles and to project a hopeful confidence to the world that the photographer was criticized for falsifying the truth.

•

Yet, when my neighbors apply too much lipstick and rouge to real life—calling captive wartime prostitutes "comfort women" and the single moms who now rent out their bodies "female hygiene agents"—their determination to deodorize embarrassment can smell to unsympathetic outsiders like nothing but a way to stink up the whole neighborhood.

•

Keeping up appearances, my neighbors might reply, is not the same as denying what's beneath. It's simply a way of placing the needs of the whole before those of the self.

PARTS AND THE WHOLE

"Think of yourself as being onstage all the time," a *yakuza,* or Japanese gangster, told a reporter for *The New Yorker* in 2012. "It's a performance. If you're bad at playing the role of a *yakuza,* then you're a bad *yakuza.*"

•

When uniforms don't broadcast what role you're playing, subtler signs must suffice. A Japanese businessman sports a company pin on his lapel; a woman from the entertainment quarter carries herself with a confident stride and a direct gaze that let you know that she's not just a regular woman with a sense of style.

•

That old man in a baseball cap is telling you he no longer has to work. That gangster who hands you his business card, complete with e-mail address and fax number, is ensuring there's no uncertainty about what part he's taken on in the collective script.

•

I hear a woman's voice in the street and honestly don't know if it's the wife I've known for more than thirty years or a stranger—so perfectly are my neighbors taught to speak in a single voice, with the same cadences.

·

This doesn't mean that people in Japan are less individual than elsewhere. Their tastes and passions are as wildly divergent, as unpredictable, as their looks and voices may not be. When I return to California, I sometimes feel I'm stepping into a world in which everyone longs to be distinct—"themselves"—and yet many political positions and interests and inclinations can seem all but interchangeable.

·

"When you are all in your robes," the Zen teacher Shunryu Suzuki told his students in San Francisco, "I can see you individually."

·

We have a self, the Buddha asserted, and we don't have a self. We live simultaneously on levels both subtle and gross.

For a maître d' at an elegant restaurant to don black tie is not pretentious; it might be pretentious for him not to do so, as if putting himself before the role he's been asked to play.

Playing a part is, deep down, about seeing yourself as a part, a tiny part of a much larger whole that, if you play your part perfectly, can be greater than the sum of its parts.

"I pretended to be somebody I wanted to be," said Cary Grant, "until finally I became that person. Or he became me."

OUT OF TIME

The most forward-looking place I've encountered in Japan is also, intriguingly, the one most rooted in the past. The first time I stepped onto Naoshima, a long-forgotten island in the quiet Inland Sea, I could hardly believe what I was not seeing. I followed a long, silent path beside the great still blue plate of the water and came to what looked like a Space Age booth of glass and concrete in a deserted parking lot.

I parted with some money and then followed a long empty driveway to a series of passageways culminating in a tall concrete all-but-imprisoning windowless tunnel. Then I arrived at a small chapel that was simply a small square room, empty, with pews around every wall. In the roof a perfect square had been cut out, so I sat down and looked up. I could see a very black crow bisecting the blue. Vapor trails, a fleece of clouds. Nothing but blue again.

James Turrell, born to a conservative Quaker family in California, has constructed such Skyspaces in many places across the globe, but nowhere is he revealed to be a Japanese artist quite so movingly as on this rough backwater known as "Honest Island." Just around the corner from his installation, I slipped off my shoes, as at a temple, and walked through a large room, an antechamber of a kind, that was entirely empty.

In the inner sanctum beyond, a set of five Monet

water lilies gleamed against white walls. Illuminated only by natural light, they came, as the afternoon darkened, to resemble ghostly Rothkos. Then I walked back to the Turrell, and saw how his exploration of light began to explain the Monets. Then I returned to the Monets, and saw how the Frenchman's rectangles matched the square that Turrell had used as a frame for the sky.

A museum that worked as a choir does, each voice heightening and deepening the others: I'd never seen a place like this. One in which there's only one way to enter—and the formidable gray twenty-first-century concrete feels anonymous, until you realize that it's drawing all your attention to the light at its end. An entire museum built underground, so it barely disturbs the tree-covered hills all around, and what you're getting is not just something to see, but eyes with which to look.

Even the simple, small café in the Chichu Museum highlights a single blond-wood bench in front of a long horizontal window, revealing the great blue expanse of the sea. Nature, you realize, works in canvases as much as any artist might; installations are everywhere if only you have eyes to see them.

The story of Naoshima is well known by now. During the economic boom of the 1980s, the Fukutake Publishing Company, based in the nearby town of Okayama, bought large swatches of the impoverished, remote island (the northern half is given over to a Mitsubishi smelting plant). Specializing in text-books, Fukutake initially opened a cultural and educational center on a Naoshima beach, complete with yurts. Then the Osaka architect Tadao Ando, a former boxer, was invited to create a museum (tucked, almost invisibly, into the hillside) in which guests could stay, allowing them to walk late at night among the artworks as if the pieces were their neighbors. Every division between their lives and the art around them dissolved.

Then he constructed a secret set of rooms on top of the mountain above the museum, erected around an oval reflecting pool and attained only by hidden monorail. At night, you can see great stretches of water and the silhouettes of islands, the lights of boats tracing silent patterns in the dark. Then he built two hotel structures on a beach, but without television (even Internet reception can be spotty there). The result is that guests are moved to sit out on their terraces and attend to the beauty of blue water and blue sky they otherwise sleepwalk past.

Naoshima, I quickly saw, is essence of Japan. Every last detail is curated, and all the museum guards are silent and young, dressed in white. You're not allowed to use pens in the museums—a worker will quietly hand you a pencil if necessary—and there's usually only one way to pass through an Ando corridor. Yet all the immaculate spaces effect a single transformation: erasing the boundaries between out there and in here. After I exited the Chichu, I saw two black-clad Japanese along the road, and wondered if they were an installation, too. I returned the minute the place opened the next morning and spent four hours looking at just the Monets and the Turrells (there's only one other room in the whole large space). Every moment, these pieces shifted as the sun moved across the sky.

The word that its overseers use for their project in their English-language promotional literature is "reactivate." Their mission is to reactivate old villages and villagers that have been left behind by the industrial revolution. Their goal is also, clearly, to reawaken the senses of everyone who visits, to remind us how much there is to see, if only we attend. In the sixteenth-century village of Honmura, an easy walk from the Chichu, old wooden houses have been shaken awake with a huge Statue of Liberty, an enigmatic rock, a pond on which one hundred twenty-five colored LED digital counters keep flashing.

The result is that more and more people from modern Tokyo—or Milan or the West Village—come to visit this old place, and the old place itself feels new. Longtime residents no longer have to quit their homes; they can restore them instead, develop gardens. And what all the art—of a piece—across the island is doing is reactivating the classical principles of Japan: simplicity, clarity and emptiness. On one cliff above the waves, Hiroshi Sugimoto has hung a framed black-and-white photograph of the horizon;

as seasons pass, Nature and the spray all around apply their own touches to the piece.

I'd long begun to feel that Naoshima, the last word in cool among worldly collectors of exquisiteness, was as pure an expression of ancient, ancestral Japan as I'd seen outside a three-hundred-year-old inn. And then I went to some of the other islands that have become part of the constantly expanding project. I saw a museum built in the ruins of a century-old copper refinery on a rough island of eggplant patches, with onions hanging outside its walls, its population forty-nine (average age almost seventy). I heard the kind of rural speech, amidst hilltop shrines and half-tended fields, that is the equivalent of Shakespearean English, with contemporary installations all around.

And I slipped into the Teshima Art Museum, which consists of nothing but an empty white cave of sorts, two hundred feet long at its deepest, with an oval opening in the ceiling at one end, another oval at the other. The only things to see were the few other visitors, silent, and some droplets of water coaxed out of tiny openings in the ground by a female artist, Rei Naito, from Hiroshima.

Somehow, shockingly, tears pricked at my eyes after a few minutes in the silence. I realized how the ovals in the roof of this womblike space recalled the oval pool around which I was staying. I noticed how this space rhymed with the Turrell opening in the sky, on the neighboring island, but in a softer and more feminine key, the two openings allowing me to see different scenes from wherever I sat. I watched a light drizzle falling against the trees, the sky change color. A young woman lay down on the floor, silky black hair fanning out against the white.

The effect was not conceptual, but dazzlingly sensual; there was nothing to think about, only to feel. One result—so Japanese—was that I was bound together within a community of strangers; we were not in our own heads, but in some shared encounter. Which century had we ended up in? I couldn't say, and perhaps it didn't matter. Really, we were just out of time altogether. In a chapel of contemplation, you simply bow before what you see. Everything was here, where there was almost nothing to be seen.

AT THE COUNTER

NO BED FOR THE NIGHT

The best place to stay on a crowded night in Japan is a love-hotel: less costly than a business hotel, it's appointed with amenities in every room—karaoke systems, high-tech showers, mini–dance floors— that you'll never find in a Four Seasons.

•

On official maps of Tokyo, love-hotels are marked out by blank spaces. Other maps show you nothing but where the wild things are.

•

Japan is the land of the bento box. Portions are small, and divisions absolute. Everything is in its place— right down to the condiments—and no sauce slops over the side, as it might in a tiffin box in India.

•

The term "love-hotel" is said to have been coined in Japan, where the establishments (traditionally designated by an upside-down jellyfish) have been around for three centuries or more. Relatively recent Japanese terms for them—"motel" and "boutique hotel"—remind you that knowing you don't speak the language is far safer than thinking you do.

•

You can tell a Japanese love-hotel by its theme-park architecture—suggesting a neglected, secondhand version of Sleeping Beauty's castle—and by the prices (for three hours or all night) broadcast outside its entrance, and by the curtained parking lots.

•

You can also tell it by its name: the Hotels Labia, Pasha, Listo and Brown Made are unlikely to offer conference rooms or babysitting facilities.

•

The largest red-light district in the country, with three thousand establishments pushed into a Tokyo area barely five hundred yards wide and two hundred yards long, is called "Kabuki-cho." Formerly the site of more official theatrical performances, it has a name that can be translated, rather perfectly, as "Playland."

•

We sometimes say that love-hotels look like Las Vegas, but really what's truer to note is that Las Vegas is our loudest taste of the "Playland" to be found in every city in Japan. The idea that what plays in Las Vegas stays in Las Vegas is the first principle of Japan's "water world," or entertainment quarters.

•

The basic rule of a regular Japanese hotel is that its public spaces will be as grand and often gilded as its private spaces (the rooms themselves) are functional and bare. A love-hotel tidily reverses this, by offering you no public space at all—only a half-hidden counter under which you push your cash and from which you receive a key—and the most extravagantly baroque private spaces.

•

In choosing rotating mattresses, glass-bottomed bathtubs and beds shaped like pineapples, the space shuttle *Columbia* or even, impressively, Queen Elizabeth II's coronation carriage, a married couple in search of privacy is simply choosing a self that belongs neither to home nor to the streets.

•

A Japanese man may spend all night—for fifteen dollars—in a "comic café" offering him unlimited XXX videos and then, in the words of the house-tidying expert Marie Kondo, cover the eyes of his teddy bear before throwing it away.

●

This doesn't mean that emotions or passions are different in Japan; only that sentiments attach themselves to different objects.

●

"The Japanese are the easiest students we have," the director of an English-as-a-second-language school in California tells me. "They never make any problems; they're ideal guests. But they're also the ones who need the most hand-holding."

●

"The Japanese are the most polite, accepting guests we have," a worker tells me in a super-luxe hotel in Marrakech. "But they're also the ones who send the most letters of complaint after they get home."

●

The Japanese are so committed to hard work, we sometimes overlook their rare gift for having fun. "To divert one's self seems, indeed, the purpose of Japanese existence," wrote Lafcadio Hearn, after years in Japan; his colleague, the English professor Basil Hall Chamberlain, after decades in Tokyo, called his adopted home "the most holiday-loving of nations."

●

If shame is social rather than, say, sexual, however, it matters less what you do than what you're seen to be doing.

●

On a jam-packed train at 11:00 on a Saturday night, a glamorous woman in her early forties with permed hair, black shirt and a short black skirt, not to mention a wedding ring, sits beside a handsome guy of around the same age, in suit and open-necked white shirt.

For a second, she hooks her finger under his wrist; he rubs the sheer surface of her black chiffon sleeve, as if checking its texture. Then he slips out at the next station, and she extracts her smartphone.

IN YOUR DREAMS

Japan abounds in fantasy spaces in part because the press of reality is so insistent. Theme parks are the confessionals of a culture that doesn't make so much of guilt, but remains in crying need of Sundays.

•

Since context determines content in Japan, you can imagine yourself to be anyone—anywhere—for a moment, so long as you accept that you can't be what or where you choose most of the time.

•

Living in California, in New York City, I felt that reality was plastic and could be bent in the direction of my dreams. Coming to Japan, I learned that its language doesn't have a future tense, but the present tense can be tweaked in any number of ways.

•

Identities are fluid, flexible in Japan, perhaps because reality is not. And in a culture based upon impermanence, you can give yourself up to any disguise, because it doesn't last.

•

How you enjoy Japan will depend in large part on how you take the two-dimensional quality that shimmers over so much of daily life, the "Cinderella Station" that dominates one whole area in a chic department-store, the "Dream-Fueling Station" at Universal Studios Japan. For some this will always speak of a hole in the heart, an absence; for others, it's the no-nonsense, practical response of a culture that deals with illusions by marking out a place for them.

•

If Japan is becoming more "American," the challenge lies not in the fact that the average height of a fourteen-year-old Japanese boy shot up by more than seven inches between 1948 and 1978 but in the fear that his ambitions and expectations may have risen accordingly.

•

When my wife walked out of her marriage at thirty-one, seeking a freer and more imaginative life, she was becoming an American in a much more fundamental way than when she married me.

We marvel at the tininess of devices and spaces in Japan; we fail to recognize the compactness of dreams. My friends in Japan are less inclined to try remaking the world than simply to redecorate its corners.

In the 1990s, scientists living in the United States won forty-four Nobel Prizes, while those working in Japan—with a population and funding roughly half as big—received just one. Yet, in the same period, Japan applied for far more patents than any other nation on the planet.

A forgetful son on his way to the Buddha was asked by his mother to bring back a relic of the revered teacher. Belatedly recalling his promise just before he arrived home, the man chanced to see a dead dog lying along the side of the road. He snatched up a tooth from the corpse's mouth and presented it to his mother as belonging to the Buddha. The old woman, moved, prayed and prayed to the object with such devotion that, it's said, the decaying tooth began to glow. It thus became as priceless as any true relic of the Buddha's might have been.

I devoured the country's classic novels when first I arrived in Japan, and long tracts on the national economy; I steeped myself in poems and memoirs and literary treatises. But one day I was browsing through Oscar Wilde and I found the line "The true mystery of the world is the visible, not the invisible." It was a typical Wilde-ism, inverting the expected so as to make an impression and couching an observation about society in a wit half borrowed from Thoreau. Then I read something else: "It is only the intellectually lost who ever argue." So much of my new home lay in that simple provocation.

With his insistence on Individualism, his delight in self-advertisement, his unrelenting ironies, Wilde did not seem an obvious guide to Japanese life. Yet he was born one year after Western ships sailed into Japan, opening up the islands after more than two centuries of almost entire seclusion. He came of age just as Japonaiserie began flooding into Europe; suddenly van Gogh was painting Hiroshiges, Manet and Lautrec were experimenting with flattened perspectives and bright colors. More deeply, Wilde saw the folds within emotions and knew that social life was a theater where the emotions are very real.

And as soon as Wilde began bringing Japanese

principles into the West, Japan began turning with reverence to Oscar Wilde; my neighbors most value their own things after these come back to them with foreign stamps. Towards the end of World War II, kamikaze pilots—most of them young humanities graduates from Japan's best universities—started penning poems as if in the shadow of Wilde. "The pain of love," reflected one, "is happiness itself." Another wrote, "Strolling in the dusk with my comrades, we dream of beautiful pastures and orchards."

The prime minister in 1941, Fumimaro Konoe, had published a translation of Wilde while at Kyoto Imperial University; the novelist Junichiro Tanizaki schooled himself in the works of the renegade aesthetician from Dublin. Soon after the war, Japan's most assertive novelist, Yukio Mishima, published a book whose title—*Confessions of a Mask*—was pure Wilde, as were its sentiments: "It is precisely what people regard as my true self that is a masquerade."

If you want to understand Japan, I grew tempted to tell friends, fling this book aside and spend time instead with ten precepts from the undercover Transcendentalist who saw that fashion was a way of concealing the hurts and hopes you were too shy to show to the world.

•

"You came to me to learn the Pleasure of Life and the Pleasure of Art," Wilde wrote to his young friend Bosie in 1897. "Perhaps I am chosen to teach you something much more wonderful, the meaning of Sorrow, and its beauty."

•

"I adore simple pleasures," he observes in *The Picture of Dorian Gray.* "They are the last refuge of the complex."

•

"Some things are more precious," it's asserted in the same text, "because they don't last long."

•

"Beauty, real beauty," Wilde also notes in *Dorian Gray,* "ends where an intellectual expression begins."

•

"To be modern," it's said in *A Woman of No Importance,* "is the only thing worth being nowadays."

"Nothing is so dangerous as being too modern,"
we read in *An Ideal Husband*. "One is apt to grow
old-fashioned quite suddenly."

"Consistency," Wilde declared in an essay, "is the last
refuge of the unimaginative."

"Life is far too important a thing," we hear in *Lady
Windermere's Fan*, "ever to talk seriously about."

"And out of the bronze of the image of *The Sorrow
that Endureth For Ever*," Wilde sighed in a poem,
"he fashioned an image of *The Pleasure that Abideth
for a Moment*."

THE 2.5-DIMENSIONAL CHARACTER

The police force in Japan is represented by an upbeat orange fairy named Pipo-kun. The nuclear industry has presented itself to the world through a perky cartoon character called Pluto-kun. The Self-Defense Force is given a pretty face by a pink sea cucumber (replacing, in late 2018, dimpled, saucer-eyed Prince Pickles).

•

There were, in 2016, ninety-two such mascots in Osaka prefecture alone, including two dogs to represent tax departments, and a caped, flying hot-water bottle.

•

The last time I checked, Kumamon, a red-cheeked, lovable cartoon bear who's the mascot of Kumamoto Prefecture, had more than eight hundred thousand followers on Twitter, not many fewer than the Japanese prime minister.

•

Japanese cartoons are as popular across the globe as Japanese actors and leaders are not. Yet Japanese cartoons are based on strange caricatures of the West.

●

When my daughter, in her mid-thirties, makes a birthday card for her five-year-old niece, she spends hours over an exquisite drawing of a little Japanese girl. But since this is a manga drawing, she takes pains to give the Japanese girl blond hair and large Western eyes.

●

During the war, the Japanese referred to B-29 planes as "B-san," meaning "Mr. B." As if the planes had minds of their own. Deferring to forces larger than oneself is a large part of how Japan carries itself, seeing the advantage of waiting to pushing ahead.

●

"Now, Life Is Living You," says the large sign in English outside the big temple that greets you as you proceed one block north from Kyoto Station.

●

On Naoshima, my wife and I had to ride a private train up to our room; within moments, Hiroko had dubbed the vehicle "Tom." Suddenly the green six-seat contraption that rattles up and down a hill, a single lamp at its front, had as much character and warmth as a beloved train-set, and we were being careful with it and looking out for Tom's arrival as fondly as if we were awaiting a small nephew.

•

Returning from our trip, I noticed that the photos Hiroko had taken of stuffed animals were far more full of feeling and poignancy than the pictures she took of friends and family. The humans, after all, always flashed peace signs and put on smiles, as if to render themselves generic.

•

My neighbors think nothing of flocking to a station to wave to a train that's being taken out of service, bringing flowers or presents for the carriages—or sending a teddy bear on a journey if they can't make the trip themselves. A school of local thought holds that "mountains and rivers, grasses and flowers, can all become Buddhas."

•

At the midsummer Festival of the Dead, Obon, I visit Kyoto's central cemetery, lit with twenty thousand candles—one at every headstone—and find two life-sized cartoon characters being led around by a woman of around twenty and a slightly older boy, both in black gowns. One of the walking creatures represents the Buddha, I'm told with a giggle, one a book of sutras.

·

When foreigners arrive in Japan, they sometimes remark—as I did, in 1985—that the people around them look like robots. This may be less because the Japanese are so machinelike and dependable than because inanimate things in Japan possess so much spirit and life.

·

The people around you on a Japanese train are often strikingly poker-faced and self-erasing. Yet the cartoon figures in the books they're carrying have bulging eyes and sport blaring colors, their ejaculations delivered in block capitals rife with exclamation points, the equivalent of "POW!" and "ZAP!!!" and "WOW!"

Japan imported its first robot from the United States in 1967; within twelve years, it had fifteen times more industrial robots in operation than did the country that inspired it.

•

In 1980, Fujitsu opened a factory where robots manufactured robot parts; today, a hotel in Nagasaki is staffed by one hundred and eighty robots. That state-of-the-art convenience has grown so popular that sister hotels are springing up across the country.

•

A puppet, the novelist Tanizaki pointed out, may actually be truer to life than an actress, precisely because (in public at least) the latter is encouraged to be so wooden and remote. "The classic beauty was withdrawn, restrained, careful not to show too much individuality," he wrote. "A more distinctive, more colorful figure would only have ruined the effect."

•

As I ride the elevator up in a crowded department-store, I notice that the machine itself is saying much more, announcing the floors, than anyone around me.

•

Even the murderous Aum Shinrikyo cult, which killed thirteen people by planting sarin gas in the Tokyo subway system, had its own "Anime Division."

BETWEEN THE *TORII* GATES

This belief in 2.5-dimensional characters, as the Japanese phrase has it—cartoon figures who seem alive, living people who present themselves as cartoon characters—sounds curious until you recall that in the Shinto universe every last piece of dust and vegetable is believed to have a spirit.

•

Kazuo Ishiguro's novels derive much of their power from the fact that they're haunted by not-quite-human creatures and walking shadows. Clones, dragons and what my neighbors might call "demi-humans" are everywhere in his work, hovering in our midst to remind us that we live in many realms at once.

•

People down the road from me pray to trees.

•

It's often noted how Japanese Buddhism has influenced the modern world, everywhere from the Zen reductions of sushi bars to the *wabi-sabi* aesthetic of white-on-white hotels. But the culture's most striking spiritual export these days is Shinto: the elevator-riding walruses and smiling blades of grass that animate Hayao Miyazaki's Oscar-winning movies, the way "decluttering guru" Marie Kondo advises you to ask your one-piece if it's "sparking joy."

●

Anime is the natural expression of an animist world.

●

"Take care of things," as the Zen teacher Shunryu Suzuki said, "and things will take care of you."

●

When one of his Western students was having trouble cleaning toilets, Suzuki suggested she speak to the toilets as if they were her friends, telling them how happy she was to get the chance to look after them. It worked.

AT YOUR DISPOSAL

Japan is the spiritual home of the service industry: the wish to serve—and to be industrious—sits at the heart of a culture of shared obedience.

•

"If a fisherman sees you emerge from the ocean after swimming," a German visitor to Japan in 1910 observed, "he will quickly remove the sandals from his feet, bow and place them before you in the sand so that you do not have to walk down the street barefoot."

•

In a mosh pit at a twenty-first-century punk concert in Osaka, I join a group of kids who are flinging themselves headlong in every direction, to set off what looks to be a riot. Young men in uniforms pass silently between our flying bodies, carrying large bags for us mock-hooligans to throw our trash in.

•

I order some stationery from a bookshop—Japan insists on using paper a centimeter or two longer than "international size"—and some unknown bodhisattva packs my order in copies of *The New York Times* so that, when I unpack my booty, I can enjoy the wrapping as much as the item I ordered.

•

The next time I place the same order, I get pages of *The Chronicle of Higher Education*.

•

It's my wife's birthday in a stylish, twenty-dollar-a-person, six-table Italian restaurant in the basement of a mini-mall in Kobe, so the sweetly smiling waitress brings out a yogurt sorbet on a plate, with one elegant candle placed in a piece of pastry—"Happy Birthday" written in chocolate around the outside—and then whips out a retro white Polaroid box camera and cries, *"Chee-zu!"*

She snaps twice, and her boss, a smoother woman in her early forties, sets a transparent cube on the center of the table, which I take to be a miniature travel alarm clock. As she turns a golden key, a laser image at its center starts revolving while "Happy Birthday to You" plays three times.

After an avocado milk shake is served in a micro-goblet to each one of us—on the house—the first waitress returns with two tiny laminated

Polaroid pictures for us to take home, a memento of the meal.

In the bathroom, I notice before departing, is a basket of FRESH MORNING toothbrush sets, allowing every customer to go back out into the world renewed.

·

"In a good democracy," a character in Oscar Wilde observes, "every man should be an aristocrat."

·

Japan is also the spiritual home of that preemptive kind of service known as convenience, often delivered by automated devices that seem to be doing our thinking (or our living) for us.

·

There are more than 5.6 million vending machines in Japan—the highest number per capita on the planet—and there are more than fifty thousand convenience stores, including convenience stores that deliver, two-story convenience stores, convenience stores just for the elderly.

·

In the United States, convenience stores are known as places for holdups and no-hopers; in Japan, they're the places you're advised to go in the event of assault or threat, the safest space in the public domain.

•

The ultimate convenience is, of course, uniformity. Every convenience store looks like every other; when I rent a car abroad, I always request a Japanese car, because a Nissan, a Honda, a Toyota all function in exactly the same way, their controls virtually indistinguishable.

•

When convenience is applied to smiles and emotions, however—when people deliver "Welcome"s as reliably as machines—we lose track of how many dimensions our life really has.

•

A bar in Japan will tell you exactly how many minutes of groping a hostess you get for your sixty bucks.

•

Amazon Japan will send Buddhist priests to your door—the service is called "Obo-san bin" or "Mr. Monk Delivery"—to perform funeral chants and other postmortem services at a third the going rate. (They'll also offer you a Buddhist name for the deceased at a fifth the usual price.)

•

The company Family Romance employs fourteen hundred actors to pretend to be family members for clients who are going through hard times. Its boss has acted as a husband to one hundred women, and as a young girl's father for months on end; one of his workers played a wife to one man for seven years. Another such company, Support One, sends actors to offer apologies on a client's behalf, to pretend to be a betrayed wife, to act as an inconsolable friend.

•

Foreigners sometimes balk at accepting such fake relationships—until they're presented with one of Asia's most beloved recent exports, the "girlfriend experience."

•

Japan has a sharp-edged sense of what can be perfected—gizmos, surfaces, manners—and of what cannot (morals, emotions, families). Thus it's more nearly perfect on the surface than any country I've met, in part because it's less afflicted by the sense that feelings, relationships or people can ever be made perfect.

•

"If you do your work cheerfully," Robert Baden-Powell instructed future Boy Scouts in his 1908 manual, *Scouting for Boys,* "your work becomes much more of a pleasure to you, and also if you are cheerful it makes other people cheerful as well, which is part of your duty as a scout."

•

Or, as Reese Witherspoon, playing a perky softball player in the lamentable movie *How Do You Know* has it, "If you do anything halfway, you'll only be half happy!"

•

Impeccable service, however, imposes demands and expectations on the customer as well. My local train in Nara now features announcements in English,

Chinese and Korean, as well as in Japanese, reminding us, every few stations, "In order not to bother other customers, please show good manners and create a comfortable atmosphere." We're told to scrunch up to make room for more passengers on the bench, not to wear shoulder bags or backpacks, not to walk while using devices, not to talk on the phone, always to keep an eye out for "suspicious articles and behavior."

●

"Do not stand in this area" is marked out (in large English letters) at the bottom of a platform elevator. Out on the streets, a huge banner, as if to guide kindergartners, warns, again in English, "Many Crowds Are Coming. Let's Walk in Line."

●

Perfection, in fact, is part of what makes Japan wonderfully welcoming to foreigners, and unyieldingly inhospitable, deep down.

●

In war, the Japanese readiness to follow every order to the last degree—and beyond—can make its people as brutal and inhuman as, in the 7-Eleven, they're unendingly sweet and obliging.

I'd truly come home, I thought as I walked across the lawn in the chill, gray morning. Not just because of the severe, unsmiling buildings all around and the dense hills, but mostly because of the human factor. Everyone I passed, as in my neighborhood in Japan, acknowledged me in some way, with a sign of respect, and every last one was well pressed, immaculate and, in fact, in uniform. When I spoke to them, they listened; there was an alertness I wasn't accustomed to when I tramped across other such places. The older souls seemed sensitive, uncommonly responsive to the needs of others: one of them, noticing I was flagging in the late afternoon, said, "Let's cancel our plans and just have a quiet dinner at home."

It was like being back at English boarding school, I thought at first: the young men in their serious costume, saluting every uniformed teacher they passed; the fact that everyone was known by last name, and was keenly aware whether he (it was mostly "he"s) was 246th or 247th in class. The room inspections and group exercises and waking up at dawn. "Sir"s and "ma'am"s to everyone before communal lunches in the huge medieval hall, and sports to be played every afternoon.

But it was something deeper and more heartening that made West Point, the United States Military Academy, feel unexpectedly like home, a perfect translation of the life I know in Japan: the courtesy, the sense of order—held up by an unbudging sense of hierarchy—the devotion to tradition and, most of all, the everyday humanity. People weren't spinning off in different directions here, lost in their own plans or orbits; they were brought together into a unit—a sense of fellowship and community—that spoke for a commitment to something larger than themselves.

Not everyone is happy to hear a country likened to a military academy; visitors sometimes complain that Japan is "fascistic" and made for war, and it's not always easy to contest that. It's no surprise that Baden-Powell combined a military ideal with a vision of innocence in creating his Boy Scouts after watching, from afar, Japan's victory over Russia in 1905. But what struck me, in the wake of thirty years of traipsing around Yale and Stanford and Claremont and Brown, was that the kids I met at West Point were wide-awake, spirited and unjaded—un–full of themselves, in fact—in a way I hadn't encountered anywhere except, perhaps, Japan.

"I've never seen less-depressed kids," wrote a reporter from *Rolling Stone* who had been keen not to write about West Point until he was given free rein by his hosts to see or say anything he wanted. I came upon his words after my first trip to the academy. Before a return trip, I read how David Lipsky, who had not found such happiness at Harvard or the University of Georgia or thirty-three other colleges he'd visited, had gone to West Point for a few weeks and been so disarmed that he'd ended up following cadets through all four years of their lives there. "It turns out that dressing like everyone else, sharing identical experiences, and being told you're on a mission of importance to the whole country does wonders for the teenage soul," he concluded.

And not just the teenage soul. At other colleges I visit, most of the professors I meet go off on long lectures about their specialized fields, as if they and their topics are the center of the world. I wasn't prepared, before West Point, for a soulful colonel who told me he was a Buddhist at heart, though his uniform, he conceded, made it hard for him to live up to such a claim. For the one who led me around the cemetery on campus, recalling all the friends and colleagues and students who'd died for a cause no one could easily figure out. For the beautiful, tall young blonde Californian officer—currently "deployed" in the English Department—who strolled in with her wife, a navy officer who had spent a year in Yemen.

This doesn't seem to go with a place I explain through Oscar Wilde. But Wilde, like Japan, lives on because he was never what popular image led one to expect. So, too, with West Point. It was startling to encounter a colonel who kept a large picture of the Qa'aba on his wall, a present from a friend in Saudi Arabia; or the one who told me with ill-disguised pride how he'd invited not just Noam Chomsky but

Chomsky's daughter to the academy, to speak for peace and to challenge almost everything the cadets were learning. When I was a guest judge one year at the *Academy Idol* competition—West Point's version of *American Idol*—I was taken aback by the brawny teenage cadet who chose to act out a dialogue between two high-pitched girls in *A Midsummer Night's Dream,* as by the classmate who elected to play out all the "rude mechanicals" in that same play ("I played Snug the Joiner in high school," whispered the friendly lieutenant-colonel next to me, an expert, he later admitted, at spotting roadside explosives in Iraq).

Of course, West Point raised questions, difficult questions, in one who reflexively hates conflict and thinks of American foreign policy as an exercise in deadly quixotism; Japan often throws me off, too, by offering values and priorities the opposite of the ones I think I admire. But I'm struck at how the English and Philosophy Departments are twinned at West Point—plays aren't mere texts for these kids—and how the seriousness of their sense of purpose makes, at times, for wild hobbies and private pursuits.

And the absence of irony, the unembarrassed sincerity with which kids there speak of "selfless service," the way that being part of a well-drilled team can liberate the self in certain ways: each time I returned to that serious, playful campus, I learned a little more about how to function, how not to feel foreign, in my home in Nara.

"I realized," Lipsky concluded, "that nobody at West Point was worried about sounding original or being entertaining . . . and I understood the immense freedom this gave them." Though competition is tough at the academy, he also registered how, on a forced march, cadets lift each other up or hang back if teammates are flagging. Communal identity—like responsibility—is one of the main things they have to master. "There's all these pressures we don't have to worry about," one member of the thin gray line told Lipsky. "In a sense, life here is easy. . . . Everything is very structured for you."

I was tickled to note that the book in which Lipsky delivered a note-perfect description of so much that surrounds me in Japan was called, in honor of a comment about West Point from Teddy Roosevelt, *Absolutely American*.

LOOKING FOR A "YES"

In Japan, manners are seen as a way to be self-possessed and other-possessed at the same time.

•

Iago in Japan is simply ego, the readiness to throw a whole exquisitely designed mechanism into chaos by focusing on one small part of it.

•

"I've heard it said," says a Zen abbess (from San Francisco), minutes after we meet, "that Japan is a land of twins." A perfect way, I thought, of catching the Japanese habit of thinking of other as self, and trying to minimize all differences (so long as you're part of the same circle).

•

The smiles we see in Japan are, again, less an attempt to get something from us than an attempt to give something. Yet, if you come from a different kind of society, you assume that elegant design hides designs of a deeper kind, projecting your own complexity upon Japan's blank screen.

"She's friendly without ever suggesting she wants or ought to be your friend," a member of her staff says of Queen Elizabeth II. The sign outside her door, as outside all of Japan, could read, "Foreign Objects May Be Less Close Than They Appear."

·

In a Confucian world, human relations are the closest thing people have to God. So manners become a kind of sacrament. They are the way you pray before the common altar.

·

In the realm of business, or of diplomacy, Japan's refusal to be confrontational leads to what many see as "impassive aggressiveness." It's impossible to tell how much distance lies between a yes and an unwillingness to say no.

·

In the gap between obedience and acquiescence, in fact— "*Hai!*" means "I'll do it," not "I agree with it"— lies much of the bewildering brutality of the Japanese in war, and the never-ending question of how much, for example, the wartime emperor was complicit in his country's aggression, how much just unable to say no.

•

Japan remains a hierarchy dressed in the clothes of a democracy. For a foreigner, treated like a VIP and someone generic all at once, it's hard to tell whether you're outside the system or beyond the pale.

•

My neighbors, however, have the satisfaction of being part of a choir that can deliver perfect and uplifting harmonies. No single contribution is heard, but if any one of them were absent, it would be missed.

THE APPLE IN THE GARDEN

We come to Japan expecting a beautifully designed motherboard in which every part of the circuit works flawlessly. And after half a lifetime in Japan, I count on such precise procedure as if I were Japanese myself. Yet the system operates to perfection only so long as everybody knows the rules. Once the smallest malfunction (or outsider) shows up, the effect is like a concertina crash on a freeway, in which each car smashes into the one in front of it and the collateral damage spreads, unsettlingly. Japan has trained all of us to deal with everything except exceptions.

One bright November morning, the sky as punctually blue as the leaves all around are gold and scarlet and brilliantly yellow, I'm writing an e-mail to my daughter, living in Spain, when an "n" flies off my keyboard.

I dig up the number for the local Apple Service Center and dial it, to be greeted promptly by an automated voice that announces, in a language I can speak, "For English-language instructions, please press 5."

I press 5, delighted at this extra courtesy—would there be Japanese-language instructions if I called a Toyota Service Center in California?—and am greeted by a slightly less automated voice that sounds, in fact, as if it belongs to someone caught up in a typhoon. This is the role of customer service, I presume: to assure the customer of the urgency of service.

I explain a little, and the poor soul at the other end grasps the problem and locates the item I need: an English-language keyboard, made for an American-produced iBook, that can be shipped almost instantly.

"You have to install it yourself," she says, just before we finalize details.

This is not good news for someone who can barely place a cassette inside a cassette recorder—yes, I'm still using 1970s technology—without setting fire to the apartment.

"Is it easy?"

"I think so." Her voice sounds less than convinced.

"Maybe I'll think about it?" I say, putting down the phone and sending her a Japanese return of serve.

I ponder the effects of being unable to work, unable to communicate and unable to support my loved ones for the next who knows how long. Then I think of the many local friends who might be up to placing a cassette inside a cassette recorder without setting off a conflagration.

I pick up the phone again. I push 5. The same voice responds.

"I think I was just talking to you? I'd be happy to order the new keyboard."

"I'll take down some details," the angel of compassion says, "and then we'll ship it. It'll be there in three days."

Next morning, at three minutes past nine, as I try to sleep off the effects of Neil Young and his enigmatic "rock opera" *Greendale* in Osaka the previous night, the phone rings.

"Hello."

A stream of Japanese pours out, to which I answer, in a kind of Japanese, "I'm sorry. I can't understand a word."

"Apple Service Center," comes back the voice, in English. "Address?"

I give it to him; the people around me are expert and scrupulous about delivering every last purchase, but this isn't always easy in a country where addresses bear only incidental relation to the places they describe.

Seconds later, as I'm trying to shake "Cortez the Killer" from my head, the buzzer rings and I open up to see a fresh-faced delivery boy in a yellow Apple windbreaker, handing me a box.

"I'll just make sure everything's okay," I say, taking the package to my dining-room table. He shrugs off his shoes and follows me in.

"Thank you," I go on. He looks as if he'd be very happy to be done with such niceties. "Shall I just sign here?"

"Thank you," he says with evident relief. "Please give back old keyboard."

Now it's my turn to look alarmed. "I don't think I can take out the old keyboard."

He stares at me, aghast.

"No give old keyboard?"

He stands there, bereft.

"I'm getting a friend to come and change it for me."

"When?"

"Friday, perhaps. Maybe Saturday."

The prospect of waiting six more days does not exhilarate. The keyboard has been delivered three days ahead of schedule, and the transaction should have been completed five minutes ago.

He pulls out a cell phone and calls a supervisor. There's a rapid-fire exchange, and then he dials another number. He's told, I gather, to leave a message.

I invite him to sit down at the dinner table, and the two of us confront each other unhappily.

"I'm sorry," I say, in Japanese that is not gaining in translation. "I'm very clumsy about these things."

"I'm sorry," he offers. "I'm only a delivery boy."

"I'm more sorry. To keep you here on a busy day."

"I'm deeply sorry," he says, even to be alive.

We sit around in silence, waiting for the phone to ring.

"I'll go outside," he says.

I'm sorry I ever took this job, he's surely thinking;

as for me, I'm sorry I ever tried to replace my defective keyboard.

I'm also sorry I don't speak Japanese perfectly, but even if I did, I'd be unable to change the keyboard.

I'm sorry he doesn't speak English perfectly, all the more so because company rules apparently forbid him to perform the action himself.

Yes, someone has enclosed instructions in Japanese—so my friends can help me—but when I show these to the delivery boy, he looks more unhappy than ever and says, in English, "No. Only baggage."

Now he returns to the room; his boss has offered no help at all.

He places another call.

"Is it a problem if I call the Apple Service Center from here?" I try.

"No," he says, which is a problem, since "No" in this situation could mean "It's not okay," or "No, it's no problem at all!"

I take the safer option and sit there in silence as he completes his call. Then we pick up our shared silence. Another call comes and he cries, *"Hai! Hai! Hai!!!"* and looks more distraught.

If he doesn't return with a keyboard, I gather, Apple will assume he's made off with it himself.

"Is it okay for me to call the Apple Service Center now?"

"Yes," he says, which I take to be not a no.

My previous redeemer is now rewiring the destiny of another caller, so I get an even more gracious high voice, eager to be of service.

I explain the situation slowly, with polite reference to the fact that I'd never have ordered the thing if I thought I'd have to replace it myself.

Then I use the dread word "cancel."

When I'd shared this term with the delivery boy, he'd looked as devastated as if I'd announced that a nuclear bomb was on its way from Pyongyang.

"I'll look into it," comes the smiling response. "Can you hold for a moment?"

Music tinkles down the line as the delivery boy puts his hand in his back pocket and then extracts it again.

"Mr. Pico," says the voice on the far end, "I'm sorry, but unfortunately it's impossible to cancel."

"Okay. Then maybe I'll just give back the new keyboard."

"Excuse me, please. I need to ask my boss."

Music chirps and tinkles down the line.

"Mr. Pico?" I know already from the timbre of her voice that things are not getting better. "When do you think you could send back the keyboard?"

"I'm going to America in December, and I hope I can replace it then. I have a friend there who's very good with machines. Perhaps I could send it back to you when I return here in January?"

"In January?"

"I'd be more than happy to do that. I don't want to put you out."

"Excuse me, please. I need to ask my boss. Could you hold for a moment?"

The music again, back where it was five minutes ago; the plaintive exchange of pregnant glances with my new friend at the dinner table, as he puts his hands in his pockets and takes them out again.

Now, as I wait, his phone begins to shrill, perhaps making my call redundant.

"Mr. Pico," says my sweet interlocutor, "why don't you cancel the order?"

"Cancel it?"

"Yes. That is all right. Since we didn't tell you about the instructions."

"Thank you. Could you please relay that to the delivery boy? He's standing right here."

I hand the phone over to my luckless new friend, whose other deliveries are growing tardier by the minute. He nods happily as he receives official dispensation to take the new machine back to his store and return to his other duties.

"*Hai, hai,*" he says, more exuberant than I've seen him hitherto. "It's understood."

"He hasn't opened the new one, has he?" I hear the girl saying over the phone.

My guest looks stricken. "Opened it? Yes, he has."

"He's opened it?"

"Yes. To make sure it's the right one."

Now the music is tinkling into his ear. The poor boss is being consulted again. Then something happens, and the boy brightens visibly.

"Yes, yes, of course! Yes. Oh yes!"

He hands the phone back to me, in a state fairly close to delirium.

The sweet girl on the other end now sounds less sweet than at any time since we started exchanging sweet nothings. As so often, the encounter has left the man relieved, and the woman ever more frustrated.

"Mr. Pico, unfortunately, because you have opened the new keyboard, we cannot cancel the transaction. We will let you keep the old keyboard."

"Keep it?"

"Yes. Please keep the old keyboard."

"I could send it to you in January."

"Please keep it."

"Thank you. Could you explain this to the delivery boy?"

"He's still there?"

"Yes, he is."

He's now, in fact—this being Japan—one of the most longtime visitors I've ever hosted.

I hand the phone back to him, and he is confirmed in the magical blessing he's surely already been given. You can never get good news too often, I think.

"Thank you," I tell the woman.

"Thank you," she says.

"Thank you," the delivery boy says, if only for releasing him to his other, even more impatient customers.

"Thank you," I tell him.

"Sorry," he says, moving towards the door as fast as his apology allows.

"I'm sorry. I wish I could speak better Japanese."

"Sorry," he says, eager to close the door behind him.

"Sorry," I say. "Thank you."

I may not be Japanese, but I've been here long enough to know how to play the game.

I'm glad I never mentioned that one reason I'd been so ready to cancel the transaction is that, in the few hours between ordering the new keyboard and having it delivered, I've found an English-speaking Japanese technical expert only ninety minutes away who will fix the fugitive "n" on my keyboard for a mere twenty dollars.

IN THE TEMPLE

THE EMPTY ROOM

I n answer to a poll conducted in 2005 by the country's largest newspaper, the *Yomiuri Shimbun,* barely one in four Japanese answered "Yes" to the question "Do you believe in any religion?" More than 96 percent, however, admitted to participating in religious rites of some kind.

•

Shinto has no texts or doctrines; Buddhism in Japan is so much a matter of rites and recitations that for centuries no one even bothered to translate many of its canonical texts into Japanese.

•

"She told Herzog that she was not sure she believed in God," Saul Bellow writes of Sono Oguki, the Japanese lover of his eponymous character, "but that if he did she would also try to have faith. If on the other hand he was a Communist she was prepared to become one, too. Because *'Les Japonaises sont très fidèles.'*"

•

When he gives lectures in the West, I heard the Dalai Lama say in Japan, the audience tunes out the minute he starts speaking about ritual and comes to life as soon as he speaks about philosophy; in Japan, the formula is reversed.

•

The Japanese tea-ceremony—with its formal raising of the cup, the handing round of the sacramental vessel, the wiping clean with a white cloth—seems to have been inspired by the Catholic mass, which European missionaries brought into the country just as Sen no Rikyu was codifying the rites of tea. But what in the Catholic church is centered on an altar, in Japan takes place in a social circle, within a largely empty room.

•

"When one tries to discuss with [the Japanese] the problems of higher philosophy or religion, in the real sense of the term," the great-grandfather of my first cousin complained in a book he published in 1933, after visiting Japan from his home in Bombay, "one feels that their religion begins and ends in ringing the bells, twice clapping their hands and then bowing with joined hands."

Intelligence in Japan is emotional and social,
someone should have told him; analysis is as
inappropriate here as eating noodles with a knife and
fork.

"The most important things in our practice,"
said the Zen teacher Shunryu Suzuki, "are our
physical posture and our way of breathing. We
are not concerned about a deep understanding of
Buddhism."

Japanese "indifference to the Mystery of the
Universe," my cousin's great-grandfather was wise
enough to add, "is that which enables them to give
more time and to spend more energy on the solution
of the problems nearer at hand."

That same indifference binds them together, because
there's no need for individual speculation or debate

in a choir; Shinto, lacking arguments, cannot be refuted.

•

To Marcel Duchamp's blithe "There is no solution, because there is no problem," the Japanese visual artist Shigeko Kubota replied, "There is no problem, because there is no solution."

•

"To do nothing at all," as Wilde noted, "is the most difficult thing in the world, the most difficult and the most intellectual."

•

The mother of Jesus, I sometimes remember, was visited by an angel and is seen as a saint; the mother of the Buddha died at his birth. Is it any surprise that Buddhism is about learning to live with loss, while Christianity is about salvation from above?

•

Many a visitor, arriving in Kyoto in late December, notes how the Japanese flock into Christian churches on Christmas Day (for Bach and Beethoven), head to a Buddhist temple on New Year's Eve for the ceremonial ringing of a bell one hundred and eight times, to purge the sins of the year now passing—and then hurry into a Shinto shrine early on New Year's Day, to set an auspicious tone for the year to come.

●

To binary minds, this seems strange. To practical Japan, it's just about meeting different needs, akin to looking in on Mom before going off to talk business with Dad. When Buddhism arrived in Shinto Japan, the two were brought together much as a foreign prince might be married off to a descendant of the Sun Goddess.

●

The mind says, "Either/or." The spirit embraces both.

ON THE MAT

Zen is what remains when words and ideas run out.

•

What we see and smell and hear is real, it reminds us; what we think about that is not.

•

In much the same spirit, the Japanese aesthetic is less about accumulation than subtraction, so that whatever remains is everything.

•

A perfect date in Japan involves accompanying a loved one to a movie, watching the film together in silence and then, on the way home, taking pains not to talk about it.

•

Words only separate what silence brings together.

•

After embarking on a study of Zen, the American writer Peter Matthiessen wrote a four-hundred-and-forty-nine-page novel, *Far Tortuga*, that contained exactly one simile. Nothing was "like" anything else; his book aspired to give us reality unadorned.

●

The last book Matthiessen published, after a quarter-century as an ordained Soto Zen priest, was about a Buddhist meditation retreat at Auschwitz, aimed at bearing witness to suffering and remembering who we really are; the novel that resulted was almost entirely an expression of rage and lust and impatience and confusion. Its title was *In Paradise*.

●

Matthiessen's novel appeared three days after its author's death. Thus, seventy-two hours after taking in Matthiessen's obituary, readers encountered the words "Peter Matthiessen, In Paradise."

●

For Arthur Koestler, a Westerner in love with distinctions, the fact that Zen monks could be seen driving to movie houses in luxury sedans, geisha beside them, showed how unenlightened they are; for those within the tradition, it shows the opposite.

•

Is not a geisha at heart the same as any other human being? Cannot a movie house liberate one from illusions as much as any meditation hall might?

•

Screens in a Zen meditation place are pulled back at dusk, to let the mosquitoes in.

•

A monastery, for St. Benedict, was "a school for charity." A Zen temple might be called a school for clarity. The challenge in either tradition is to see how one leads to the other.

•

For a Westerner, Joseph Campbell noted in Japan, meditation may awaken a sense of divinity within; for a Japanese, it's more likely to inspire a sense of divinity inside a temple, a flower, a gnat. The person sitting still doesn't say, "I'm awake." She says, "The world is illuminated!"

＊

When my mother learned Japanese flower-arrangement in California, her (American) teacher explained that it was a kind of meditation, a training in attention. I mentioned this to a Japanese man, and he grimaced. He'd never use the word "meditation" for *ikebana,* he replied; it was a form of hospitality, of caring for a guest.

＊

"Buddhist meditation frees you from God and frees you from religion," said the singer-poet Leonard Cohen, deep into a forty-year-long Zen practice.

＊

Cohen's final album, however, was clearly addressed to God, as well as to a religious teacher. In his final press conference, late in 2016, when asked why he was shown on the album's cover holding a cigarette after claiming to have given up smoking, the sometime monk cracked a smile and said, "Some guys you just can't trust."

WORDS

More important than learning to speak Japanese when you come to Japan is learning to speak silence. My neighbors seem most at home with nonverbal cues, with pauses and the exchange of formulae. What is the virtue of speaking Japanese, Lafcadio Hearn noted, if you cannot think in Japanese?

●

A typical sentence in India—or from my friend from Mexico—begins, "No, but . . ." Every other Japanese sentence begins, *"So, so, so, so,"* or "Yes, yes, yes, yes."

●

Seventy percent of Japanese sentences, by one count, lack a subject, and 50 percent of all spoken sentences do, too.

●

Japan's foundational novel, *The Tale of Genji*, is notoriously hard to translate, because proper names are sometimes avoided, the subject of a sentence changes halfway through and speakers are seldom indicated. As the scholar of Japan Ivan Morris writes, the hard-and-fast divisions we like to maintain—between past and present, question and statement, singular and plural, male and female—don't apply. "Sometimes it is not even clear whether the sentence is positive or negative."

•

Even those sentences that do have clear beginnings in Japan generally trail off, like pen-and-ink drawings that leave most of the page open for a viewer to complete. In England, I learned to start sentences by saying, "I'm not exactly sure . . ." but in Japan the studied vagueness is not just about diffidence but about allowing room for someone else to turn an opening note into a duet.

•

Speech is dangerous in Japan, precisely because so many unspoken rules hover around it. It's generally a bad idea to use the word "you"—too intrusive—and there are said to be twenty ways of saying "I." Women are expected to refer to themselves in the third person, men not. A single verb in Yasunari Kawabata's short novel *Snow Country* is translated in twenty-nine different ways because what we would render as "I think" can in Japan mean "I remember," "I long for" or twenty-seven other things.

•

One prince in *Genji* has never been allowed to speak with his own sister except through curtains or behind a screen. Yet men in Genji's world think nothing of going to bed with women with whom they've never exchanged a word.

•

You can tell a Japanese restaurant in the Sixth Arrondissement of Paris, my wife points out, by the fact that (unlike the places run by Koreans or Chinese) it never says "Japanese" at the entrance.

•

In Japan, more than anywhere, nothing is more fatal than thinking you know what's being said. The English word "hip" in Japan refers to the buttocks, and "smart" means slender. "Naïve" is a good word in Japan, and so is "tension." A "mansion" refers to a thick-walled, modern and often small apartment.

•

A couple that got married in Nagasaki soon after the bomb was dropped on the city, Susan Southard reports, would mention the transfiguring event once, and then never again.

•

"If you think, 'I breathe,'" said Shunryu Suzuki, the Zen teacher, "the 'I' is extra."

NO WORDS

There are two silences," wrote Harold Pinter, introducing his *Complete Works*. "One when no word is spoken. The other when perhaps a torrent of language is being employed. This speech is speaking of a language locked beneath it."

•

Perhaps the most celebrated poem in Japan is Basho's gasp of delight at seeing the island of Matsushima. The whole poem consists of just the name, a gasp and two particles: *"Matsushima ya / Ah Matsushima ya / Matsushima ya."*

•

Hours after the bomb was dropped on Hiroshima, what struck a German priest was the silence, even in a grove where hundreds of survivors had gathered. No one wept or screamed; no one complained; children barely cried. Those who sobbed, sobbed silently; those given water bowed their thanks.

•

"No word," wrote Japan's Nobel Prize–winning novelist Yasunari Kawabata, "can say as much as silence."

•

"People in America would be upset," I said to my wife when she informed me that her doctor had just told her, for the first time, that she'd been suffering from a mild form of cervical cancer ten years previously (he'd told her now only because the danger seemed to have passed).

"Really?" she sang back. "I thought he was being kind!"

•

When, however, Hiroko went into the hospital for a simple infection, nineteen years later, her friends assumed she was struggling with cancer.

•

Editions of *The Tale of Genji* come with seventy closely packed pages of genealogy. But the book's author, Lady Murasaki, never mentions either her late husband or her small daughter in her diary.

•

At Kyoto's most exclusive inn, Tawaraya, its thousand-dollar-a-night rooms often the preserve of European royalty or Hollywood movie stars, many of the staff don't speak English. Finding English-fluent workers would not be hard, but part of the grace of the inn is to see that English doesn't go with shuffling feet and kimono, with seasonal delicacies and polite demurrals. The most essential things come across without words.

•

"His magnanimity was apparent to all who met him," a local guide told the American poet James Merrill of Arnold Toynbee's visit to Japan. "Never once did he reveal his true feelings."

•

In England, Japan's Western cousin, I learned that the ultimate sign of intimacy is not all you can say to a friend, but all you don't need to say.

•

The less my Japanese neighbors talk, the more room there is for surprise, and for them constantly to transcend my understanding.

•

Sometimes, in fact, my friends in Japan disarm me by not seeming eager to have the first word, sometimes by not seeming anxious to have the last.

●

"My voice gives out when I'm singing for someone I know well," says a geisha in Kawabata's *Snow Country.* "It's always loud and brave for strangers."

●

In Japan, I never forget that a great conversationalist is one who listens. The visionary theater-director Peter Brook told me he'd bring all his productions to Japan because even in his nine-hour rendition of *The Mahabharata,* without subtitles, Japanese audiences sat rapt. In L.A., where people could follow every word, they were fidgeting in their seats, whispering, barreling off to the restroom and falling asleep.

●

In the public sphere, this commitment to saying nothing may suggest a crippling caution and refusal to take the initiative. In the private, it opens up to a bottomless intimacy.

●

I used to watch Leonard Cohen and his great friend of more than forty years, the Zen teacher Joshu Sasaki-roshi, sit in silence together for long stretches, not least because Cohen spoke no Japanese and Sasaki limited English. When I visited Cohen at his home, he would take a couple of chairs out into his tiny front garden, overlooking a bed of flowers, so we could sit there for half an hour or more, saying nothing.

●

One sign that Sofia Coppola's *Lost in Translation* is a Japanese movie is the fact that the audience never hears its last, and presumably most important, sentence.

●

Another is that we don't know whether it has a sad or happy ending.

●

The first koan given in many a Zen temple is *mu*. The best translation of this is "Not one, not many, not no, not yes." It might almost be the interval between the notes out of which John Cage made his Japanese-inflected music—or the name Cage's fellow Zen student Leonard Cohen took on with his black robes: "Jikan," sometimes translated as "the silence between two thoughts."

•

Long before Cage's *4'33"*, a musical piece in which nothing was played, Shinto shrines were said to offer "silent concerts," in which wind instruments and strings assembled, and not a note was delivered.

W hat do you think you'll miss most when you leave?" a close friend from California asks me one bright autumn afternoon. We're sitting on a bench in the Deer Park at the heart of Nara, watching the holiday atmosphere of a warm November day unfold. A chic couple, dressed in black from head to toe, is batting a shuttlecock back and forth. Children play far off amidst the trees. Above a pond, the rusting leaves on the misty slopes look like something out of an old Eastern watercolor.

"Usually, people say they'll miss the food, the hot springs," my friend goes on, perhaps to prompt me. "Or the freedom of being a foreigner, able to get away with almost anything."

"I'll miss the cleanliness of the air," I say. "I don't mean just the spotless streets and the fact that everyone changes clothes every few hours, and always looks so freshly pressed and laundered. I don't mean even the shine around things, which makes you feel as if you're seeing every last surface through freshly polished glass, framed by doors and screens as in a lens.

"I just mean that people don't feel the need to smudge every moment with their signature. When it's hot, they don't say, 'It's warm enough to roast a chipmunk in the streets!' or 'Phew! It's hotter than a squirrel on a barbecue!' They just say, 'Hot, isn't it?'

in exactly the same words and exactly the same tone, so that it might be the air itself speaking, or the day. It might be no one at all."

Around us, the scene is not so different from what you might find in Hyde Park or the Jardin du Luxembourg. People everywhere stretch out and have fun in much the same way. But there is a stillness, a self-containment in every direction—so crowded and so quiet—I haven't felt even in Myanmar or Singapore.

"Every night, when I leave the health club, four or five kids at the front desk shout out, 'Take it easy. You've worked hard!' I know it's just a formula; I know it means nothing at all. But it's an attempt to sweeten the moment, to give me energy, to make every departure feel like the first step towards coming back. It suggests that something remains steady in a world of constant change."

My friend says nothing; that's one of the practices he's trained me in since we met, my third day in the country. Back home, when I tell friends that I always buy Toyotas because they're so uncomplicated and reliable—fewer features mean fewer things to go wrong—they don't always realize I'm speaking about relationships and conversations as much as about cars. When I talk of the economy of verbal and facial expressions in Japan, they may not see that stock verbal exchanges make the country go round much more than the Nikkei Index does.

We've been on the bench for more than an hour

now. The sky is slowly darkening. The deer are still grazing in the falling light. Children are beginning to collect their things to follow their parents back home. Michael will soon be moving back to California after half a lifetime in Japan.

"I suppose it's all the things you don't have to say or explain," I conclude, "that I'll miss when I'm not here," and we stand up and walk back to the station.

CROWDS

More people live within thirty or so miles of Tokyo than on the entire continent of Australia.

•

Northern Greenland, which occupies a space as large as Japan and France, combined, has a population of exactly forty.

•

Lacking space has naturally made the Japanese masters of making space—in a crowded rush-hour train, in a poem or a painting.

•

Making room for the new or different is less easy, however; in tight quarters, there's less room for taking chances.

•

The main road in Kyoto was, in the eighth century, said to be the widest in the world. As if in response, the side roads are most notable for their narrowness and intimacy. The magnitude of public spaces has made for an intricacy of private ones.

●

"The extreme physical intimacy of this society necessitates emotional reserve," writes Andrew Solomon of, in fact, Greenland. "Yes, it is true," a local woman tells him. "We are too physically close to be intimate." It's rude, she goes on, "to say to someone, even a friend, 'I'm sorry for your troubles.'"

●

In Tokyo, one building of just nine hundred and fourteen square feet stretches across twenty-one stories.

●

In Tanizaki's novel *The Maids,* set in 1937, seven or more maids share a room of seventy-five square feet. In those days, the average resident of Washington, D.C., enjoyed four hundred times more private space than his counterpart in Tokyo.

A typical Japanese convenience store is one hundred square meters in size, and stocks twenty-five hundred items. A typical page in a Japanese magazine is often no less cluttered. Emptiness in Japan becomes the luxury that grandeur is in the West.

•

My first days in Japan, I was startled at the almost overwhelming crowds that dwarf many a festival, making it difficult to move, even to breathe. Now that I live in Japan, I see that it's crowds that make the festival, much more than the spectacle itself. It's their unembarrassed gasps, the high-pitched cries of delight, the collective roar—the whole sense of being part of a large and happy unit—that gives a public celebration its warmth.

•

In Japan, a crowd is less a threat to public order than a reaffirmation of it: at a Japanese festival of thirty-two thousand holidaymakers in 1878, Isabella Bird noted, "A force of twenty-five policemen was sufficient."

As the world grows more cluttered, the spare Japanese aesthetic (of clean sushi bar and severe minimalism) grows ever more appealing. In a global Varanasi, nothing so clarifies as a bamboo flute in an empty room.

IN THE GARDEN

In Europe, a garden is something you enter, walk around in and leave behind; in Kyoto, a garden is more like something that enters you, inviting you to become as silent and well swept as everything around you.

•

Departing a Japanese garden, you hope to carry some of its pruned stillness out into the streets; the only thing you need leave behind is yourself.

•

When Chinese tourists began shaking cherry trees in Tokyo in 2017 to make picturesque backdrops for their selfies, it struck many Japanese as a kind of sacrilege; the whole point of a Japanese landscape is that it makes a schedule for you rather than the other way round.

•

What Nature does to us defines us much more, my neighbors know, than what we do to Nature.

A garden is therefore observed as a ceremony might be.

•

A Japanese psychiatrist asked every prospective patient to keep a daily journal. He consented to see each one only after all her sentences were devoted to the world outside her.

•

A Christian church generally has a roof and directs your eye towards a single cross; a Shinto shrine is often surrounded by a large expanse, so your attention is drawn to trees and grass and sky, the place where Japan's sovereign deities live.

•

"Look beneath your feet," says the inscription at the entrance to many a Kyoto temple, reminding you that Heaven can be found by looking down as much as up.

•

The running water all around tells you that you step into a Japanese garden not just to open your eyes, but to close them.

•

The pond in front of you is often kept deliberately shallow—no more than thirty inches—so below becomes a crystalline reflection of above.

•

"There's no performance," says my wife, as we sit in a Japanese garden (in California). "The trees are in harmony; none of them stands out. There are no bright colors." And the trees enfold us in a circle.

"No big light," she goes on. "Everything is hidden. That makes us calm."

•

In the English summer gardens of my youth, we exulted in a dozen brilliant colors; in Saihoji in Kyoto, there are one hundred and thirty shades of green, radiating from as many different kinds of moss.

•

Growing things in Japan are kept mostly inside the house. The garden is more liberally appointed with boulders and stone lanterns. Unmoved by wind, they bring us to stillness, and freedom from distraction.

●

That the Japanese garden is about transformation is evident from the way it makes rivers out of dry sand and turns "living curtain" hedges behind its walls into a part of the organized scene. A white-pebble courtyard creates a space as large as the heavens.

●

Silence, the running water tells you, is no more the absence of noise than health is mere freedom from sickness, or stillness an absence of movement. The richest part of life lies in the space between absence and presence.

●

Reading Shusaku Endo's novel *Silence* in a traditional Kyoto inn, Martin Scorsese noticed how the room and its garden were essentially one. The Japanese didn't need a Christian God, he realized, because streams and rocks and flowers brought local deities into the house at every moment.

When Francis Xavier came to Japan to try to carry the Gospel to its people, the Japanese he met became "the delight of my soul." But he found they quickly, reflexively, translated the word "Deus" into "Dainichi," converting the Christian God into a god of wind and rain.

On arrival in Japan, I hurried to the rock garden at the temple called Ryoanji, eager to work out whether its arrangement of fifteen stones—you can't see all of them from any one position—represented clouds in the sky or a tiger carrying her cubs across a stream. Now that I've spent time in Japan, I walk past that garden to the stone basin around the corner, whose characters, one on each of its four sides, read, "What you have is all you need."

FREEDOM FROM CHOICE

Japan is the Land of Must, I decided as soon as I set foot in Tokyo, as surely as America is the Land of Can. It's the difference between an arranged marriage, a practical affair in which, it's hoped, affection can grow and grow, and an affair of the heart, in which, too often, passions burn wildly and then peter out.

•

"Nothing sets you (or at least me) free creatively," says the untamed film director and Monty Pythonite, Terry Gilliam, "like having a set of limitations to explore."

•

Even modest restaurants in Japan often present you with a prix fixe menu. Freedom doesn't mean an abundance of choice so much as liberation from the burden of too much choice.

•

At a very elegant restaurant in Kyoto, there are only five set menus on offer, ranging in price from one hundred and twenty-five dollars to three hundred dollars each. Each person in a party of five must choose the same set, so each has to learn, as Tolstoy had it, how "freedom consists in my not having made the rules."

•

As soon as prostitution was banned in postwar Japan, the number of prostitutes (said to be roughly eighty thousand in Tokyo alone) rose sharply.

•

It took me a long time, after meeting my wife, to see that the kindest and most thoughtful thing to do in many situations was *not* to ask her where she wanted to eat or go. To take the decision myself was to free her from both the burden of choice and the responsibility that follows (knowing that, when it came to what to wear or what to eat at home, she'd extend the same kindness by making the decisions for me).

•

"To know that you are a sparrow and not a swan; or, on the contrary, a swan and not a sparrow . . . gives a great security, stability and quality of harmony and peace to the psyche," Joseph Campbell wrote in Kyoto in 1955, drafting a convocation address for his students back at Sarah Lawrence.

●

If you're always wondering what you will become, he went on, "you will soon become so profoundly implicated in your own psychological agony that you will have little time or energy for anything else, and certainly no sense whatsoever of the bliss and wonder of being alive."

●

In Japan, a son traditionally follows his father into his profession, even if that's the profession of monk or musician. Rather than choosing what he'll be good at, he aims to be good at what's chosen for him.

●

"We only escape limitation," wrote Simone Weil, "by rising up towards unity or going down towards the limitless."

●

Soon after I came to know her, my wife-to-be said, "I can't change you, so I have to change myself, since you're in many ways not so easy." I was so disarmed by this spirit of accommodation that I tried to do the same with her, changing myself to adapt to everything in her that was difficult.

Thus the history of Japan.

BEING RESPONSIBLE

I f you want condition of warm in your room,"
says the instruction manual for a Japanese air
conditioner, "please control yourself."

•

The pressures of responsibility are what make the
Japanese the strictest people I know, even as the
constant attention the pressures encourage makes
them the kindest. After the Tokyo Olympics in 1964,
modern Japan's proudest moment, one woman
hurdler who didn't win the medal she expected
took her own life. A Japanese marathoner who was
overtaken at the last moment and claimed only a
bronze did the same.

•

I arrive at my local health club to be greeted by an
elaborate red-and-blue diagram on the floor in front
of each elevator, to show me where to stand when
the elevator doors open. On arrival at the fifth floor, I
see arrows denoting which side of the stairs I should
use in walking down to the locker room. There are
ghostly outlines of feet at the entrance to the toilet,

telling me where to place the toilet slippers. Farther inside, a laminated card shows a woman deeply bowing as she reminds me not to wear my athletic shoes here.

If ever a locker is broken, another large card is hung on its front, depicting a woman offering a deep bow, accompanied by fulsome words of apology in both Japanese and English.

Meanwhile, an elderly woman moves among all the naked men, sweeping up the trash.

•

When conflict arises in Japan, it's often because one person wishes to give up her needs as much as another wishes to give up hers. Such duels of self-sacrifice leave everyone stranded in an agony of thwarted self-denial.

•

People in Japan are sometimes slow to intercede in an emergency, because they don't want to impose a debt on those they help.

•

To be part of a circle frees you from the pressure of having to make a decision. But it imposes on you the pressure of knowing that every move you make will affect everybody else.

●

When a man tried to kill the country's regent, in 1923, the village in which he was born canceled all New Year festivities, and the man who was principal at the time of the elementary school where the attacker had studied, decades before, resigned.

●

Several hours after my wife is made to wait a few minutes at the bank, there's a knock on our door, twenty minutes away by car: the bank manager, here at our distant apartment at 9:00 p.m., to offer an apology and to hand us a small gift in recompense.

●

In England, I was taught never to take anything seriously, least of all myself. When I moved to America, I was encouraged to take everything seriously, especially myself. In Japan, the people I know don't seem to take themselves very seriously—but only because they take their roles, the parts they have to play in the national pageant, very seriously indeed.

The pressures that accompany every decision leave many a foreign businessman—or Western husband—in Japan unsure of whether the person beside him is following her inclination or his own.

●

The truth is that she herself may not know—or want to know.

●

The Japanese after the war "gained a strange peace of mind," Isamu Noguchi observed in 1950. "They are as it were free, free from the responsibility of being powerful."

●

The buses in my neighborhood run on the honor system; no one seems to notice whether I pay the requested three dollars or three cents. Yet, if I pay upon entering when we're leaving the train station—or fail to pay upon entering when we're going in the direction of the train station—the driver flies into a spasm of displeasure. It's not morality that's important, but the unwritten rules.

●

Twenty miles from where I live, organized criminals invite kids to their headquarters every October to collect candy for Halloween. When a factional battle made that impossible one year, a sign came up outside the building, regretting the cancellation and announcing, "We realize this is causing great sorrow to those parents and children who looked forward to this, but next year we will absolutely hold the event, so please look forward to it."

●

After murdering (and dismembering) the English bar hostess Lucie Blackman, the Japanese man suspected of being her killer sent money to the police, through a friend, to settle all her outstanding debts.

●

"Family not send money?" my wife asks, when we hear that a train killed a pedestrian in an accident in California. "No," I say, "the family is more likely to sue Amtrak to get money out of them." She looks confused: in Japan, the family feels obliged to take financial responsibility for the inconvenience caused by a suicide, or even an accident.

•

The United States sees ten times more murders every year than does Japan. Yet Japan has been home to sixteen times more professional gangsters than the States had when the Cosa Nostra was at its peak.

•

The conviction rate of suspects in Japan is 99.85 percent (as against around 80 percent in Britain and the United States). Is this because the police are so efficient—or so reluctant to admit a mistake? Is it because the accused assume they must have done something wrong—or because they're pressured to act as if they did? Is it because prosecutors take on cases only if they expect to win—or simply because in Japan an arrested person is assumed to be guilty unless proven innocent?

•

Although at least one hundred and forty nations have abolished the death penalty, in Japan support for capital punishment runs at more than 80 percent.

Inmates—often half blind or in wheelchairs—are routinely hanged on Christmas Day, when not so many will notice, and neither they nor their families are given advance notice.

•

Inquiry, in every sense, is not encouraged in a society based on harmony. Japan is the rare society that offers no life sentences without parole.

•

I'm stunned, in a Californian ICU, that the nurses tending to my stroke-ridden mother change every day.

"I suppose they don't want the staff getting too emotionally engaged with patients who could die at any moment," I tell Hiroko.

"No," she says. "Responsibility. If something happens, they don't want any one individual to feel it's her fault."

THE BRIDGE OF HESITATION

The first sentence of Kazuo Ishiguro's second novel, set in Nagasaki just after the war, introduces us to a painter living next to a thoroughfare known as "The Bridge of Hesitation."

•

In Junichiro Tanizaki's novel *The Makioka Sisters,* set a decade earlier, the action for more than five hundred pages turns on nothing but a young woman's refusing to say yes to any proposal, and not really saying no.

•

"Whenever they had to decide whether to go out or not," Tanizaki writes of a married couple in *Some Prefer Nettles,* "each of them became passive, watchful, happy to take a position according to the other's manner. It was as if they had a basin of water balanced between them and waited to see in which direction it would spill. Sometimes the day passed without their coming to a decision."

•

That indecisiveness is fatal, because both husband and wife are unhappy in their marriage and both have taken on lovers. But neither will take responsibility for being the one to break their union, so they remain in sorrowful limbo forever.

•

As the husband says, inverting the sentiment I expect to hear elsewhere, "Each of us thinks the other is perfectly right, and that makes everything impossible."

•

"If you're always thinking of the other person first," a sister pointedly reminds her clergyman brother, always too set on doing the right thing (in Elizabeth Strout's novel *Abide with Me*), "you don't have to bother with what *you're* feeling. Or thinking."

•

Zen teachers in Japan are often invigorated by Western students, because they've chosen to engage in the practice and are not just, as are their Japanese counterparts, following family obligation. But Zen teachers in Japan are often frustrated by Western students for the same reason: they choose to move off again, as their Japanese counterparts seldom do.

•

The Japanese game of Go has only two rules, but there are more possible moves, by several orders of magnitude, than there are atoms in the universe.

•

When Japan was ushered into an arranged marriage with America after the war, it had to address, with fresh urgency, how much to follow the forward-looking way of its new partner, how much not to sweep under the carpet.

•

The theme of Ishiguro, born in Nagasaki in 1954, is always what to do with the past—how at once to respect it and to set it aside. His characteristic time is twilight, when what has recently been visible becomes as bleary as what is about to come. His first non-Japanese novel, bearing the very Japanese title of *The Remains of the Day,* centers on one postwar figure who, realizing, too late, that he failed to take responsibility in the public sphere and failed to take initiative in the private, is left in a shadowland of "If only"s.

•

Its sequel, set a generation later, is the book the Japanese novelist Haruki Murakami entitled *After Dark*—or, in postwar Japanese, *Afuta Daku*.

George Mikes begins his classic text *How to Be an Alien*—the funny, wide-eyed tale of a Hungarian coming slowly to know the upside-down ways of his new neighbors, the English—with the simple truth, "In England everything is the other way round." To Englishmen, of course, this applies even more to Japanese, the people who flip their light switches up, not down, for off, who used to count the hours backwards, from twelve to four, and who say "Yes" where we would say "No."

A book called *How to Be a Japanese* would point out that people in this looking-glass world admit to feeling happiest when they can feel sad and see a gift as less a blessing than a burden (since now they'll have to reciprocate). They traditionally wrote their names and addresses backwards (as it seems to us) and placed footnotes at the top of a page and a period at the beginning of each paragraph.

For fires or an ambulance they dial 119, and at a baseball game you hear of "two-and-three" counts.

I step into a bullet train in Osaka and see that the seats are numbered "E-D" and "C-B-A." I get off the train and walk into an elevator, to ascend from the B1 floor to the B2. Prices are described as "¥7000–3000," and bars advertise their opening hours as "9:00– 25:00." A vegetarian meal in my favorite Kyoto restaurant, Kerala, costs 50 percent more than one with chicken or beef or lamb.

"Always the left is the right side," Lafcadio Hearn noted, of the adopted home he often loved, "and the right side the wrong; and keys must be turned, to open or close a lock, in what we are accustomed to think the wrong direction." We pass a thread through the eye of a needle, Hearn recalled; the Japanese pass a needle through a thread.

"To speak backwards, write backwards, read backwards," wrote the Boston polymath Percival Lowell, in 1888, "is but the *a b c* of their contrariety. . . . From the standing of a wet umbrella on its handle instead of its head to dry to the striking of a match away in place of toward one, there seems to be no action of our daily lives, however trivial, but finds with them its appropriate reaction—equal but opposite." After writing a provocative book on Japan as America's mirror society, which, "like all mirrors gives us back left for right," Lowell turned his gaze to Mars.

In all of this, Hearn and Lowell—Mark Twain, too, and Britain's first permanent diplomatic representative in Japan ("They write from top to bottom, from right to left, in perpendicular instead of horizontal lines; and their books begin where ours end")—were following in the footsteps of one of the first foreigners to set foot in Japan, the sixteenth-century Portuguese missionary Luis Fróis. In a letter to a fellow Father, in Nagasaki, Fróis wrote, "This is a country seen in a mirror, where everything is backwards compared with Europe.

"In Europe," he went on, in a frenzy of listing all the ways in which "everything is reversed" in the East, people "of rank ride in the stern of the ship, while in wrong-way-around Japan, they ride in the prow." We "avoid vague expressions," he continued, gaining steam, "while they set high value on the ambiguous. We sew a wound where they paste a piece of paper on it. Our ink is liquid, but theirs is a lump of black stone. We write letters at great length, while they write brief ones."

On and on the list went, citing matters of etiquette and emotion and religion, and when Fróis published a book, listing six hundred and eleven ways in which Japan was Europe inverted, its title was rendered as *Topsy-Turvy*, a term that many a newcomer trots out to this day.

Every November, my local bus explodes into a chorus of deafening sniffles and coughs, of cleared throats and gagged sneezes and running noses, the last word in unseemliness, as it seems to me. But that's only because, although every Japanese carries a handkerchief, every Japanese believes that to blow your nose into something that's already unclean is the last word in unseemliness.

So, by trying hard to be polite, they affront me (and many a foreigner) with what we take to be maximal rudeness.

If, as Mikes says, "in England, everything is the other way round," Japan manages to be the wrong way round from England, without ever becoming Hungary. As my Japanese neighbors would say, "Nothing is really white-and-black."

BEHIND CLOSED DOORS

WHAT LIES WITHIN

J apan likes to present itself to the world in its collective, corporate face—in groups—and we like to see it in terms of stereotypes. Yet everything fresh, surprising and warm in Japan takes place at the level of the individual: Japan's great accomplishments may be communal, but its treasures are its constantly unexpected and passionate people.

•

Nowhere else I've been, in fact, are individuals so disengaged from the political domain; my Japanese friends assume they can no more address their leaders than they can a group of look-alike men in suits in a corporate boardroom with the doors locked and the curtains drawn. So they turn their backs on the public sphere, and make fantastic worlds out of their passions, counter-societies out of their hobbies.

•

"Success and satisfaction could rarely be sought by way of public accomplishment," writes Krista Tippett of East Germany in the 1980s. "In response, ordinary people defended and grew their inner lives defiantly."

Pragmatic to the core, my Japanese pals are happy to take four-day trips around Europe, because they know that four days of novelty can furnish forty years of memories. Experience is less important than what we make of it.

•

If they can't get to Europe, they'll find their way to a local theme-park Eiffel Tower. Even a place that we write off as "inauthentic," they realize, can arouse emotions that are entirely authentic.

•

At a Starbucks in central Kyoto, seats are lined up in a row, so you can look out at a sixth-century temple in a courtyard. At the National Museum of Modern Art, not far away, chairs are likewise set out in a line in a large empty room so you can look out at the busy streets, the girls flowing past in spring kimono, the cherry trees framing a thin canal.

•

No one married to a Japanese would ever call her "repressed." She simply has a sharp and unwavering sense of where emotion is appropriate and where not; she lives in the gap the British classicist Jasper Griffin explained to his friend Ved Mehta between denying one's emotions and choosing not to indulge them.

●

"Have more than thou showest," as his Fool advises Lear, "speak less than thou knowest."

●

Read the classic poems of Kyoto and you see that a night of love is less important than the way one anticipates it or the words with which one commemorates it. What we do with our feelings lasts longer than the feelings themselves.

●

In the most celebrated modern essay on classic Japanese aesthetics, *In Praise of Shadows,* Tanizaki extols the beauty and suggestiveness of all you can't see, because that gives the imagination, the inner world, more to work with.

●

By the time of Haruki Murakami, however, the outside world has become such a mist, a mystery, that one descends into the hypnotic passageways of an inner world that seems to lead nowhere at all.

•

Four million people pass through Shinjuku Station in Tokyo every day—it's the busiest station in the world—but many Japanese believe that hundreds remain within its bowels, unable or unwilling to come up to any of its two hundred exits. Real lives are played out under cover.

•

As many as one million people in Japan are so estranged from the outside world that they are shut-ins, living in their own heads, much like the dangerous dreamers of the Aum Shinrikyo cult, who, in Murakami's nonfiction book about them, inhabit the subterranean tunnels of delusion, working to hatch utopias.

•

On being awarded the Kyoto Prize, the artist William Kentridge was greeted by the mayor of Kyoto. The man wore a kimono that was completely plain, Kentridge noted. But when the mayor opened it up, his visitors saw that the inner lining, the part almost nobody would ever see, was fantastically embroidered.

THE FAIRER SEX

The Japanese Constitution, unlike its American counterpart, speaks explicitly of "the essential equality of the sexes," thanks in part to the Western woman who helped draft it. Having honored that on paper, however, Japan feels free to ignore it in real life.

•

In Japan, as Tiger Tanaka advises Sean Connery's James Bond upon the latter's arrival in Japan (in the film of *You Only Live Twice*), "men always come first."

•

To early Japanese, one sign of Western barbarity was the respect foreigners showed to women. Japanese gallantry had less to do with chivalry to a lady than with fealty to a lord.

•

Japan's streets are less threatening to women than those of almost any other country; but that is partly because pleasure is left to the domain of professional women, relegating their everyday sisters to the realm of duty and domestic obligation.

In traditional Japan, it was considered discourteous for a man to be too friendly to a woman, because that suggested, in the division of responsibilities, that she was a worker in the "pleasure quarters."

●

As of 2019, fewer than 1 percent of management positions in Japan are held by women. And by 2016, the majority of women in Japan who did hold jobs were engaged in "nonregular work"— sometimes temporary, sometimes part-time. Their average salaries, as of 2014, fell well below poverty levels.

●

The year after I arrived in Japan, a *Japan Times* survey found that seven in ten Japanese men refused even to consider working for a woman.

●

In a survey conducted in 2014, nine in every ten young Japanese women said that remaining single

was preferable to what they imagined marriage
to be.

•

When, after five hundred and twenty-nine pages,
Tanizaki's *The Makioka Sisters* concludes at last in a
wedding, its final sentence shows the bride on her
way to the altar, stricken with diarrhea.

•

In Sawako Ariyoshi's *The Doctor's Wife,* a twentieth-
century novel set in late-eighteenth-century Japan, a
woman is "considered past her prime" because "she
was still living with her parents at the age of twenty-
one." When a lord stops by the parents' home, it's
assumed he will enjoy their daughter after dinner;
if he does not, it will be a mark of shame to his
hosts.

•

When I arrived in Kyoto in 1987, women were known
as "Christmas cakes" if they were still unmarried at
twenty-five (since, by December 25, a Christmas cake
is too old to be of any use). Now—progress is slow—
they are known as "New Year's Eve gifts."

•

"As women," a scholar from East Asia told me, merrily, "we're so used to being put down that we're always waiting to become mothers-in-law. Then, at last, we have someone to boss over." Or, as my Japanese wife has it, having survived a marriage to a Japanese man, "He know he can anytime get new wife. But cannot get new mother!"

•

No wonder, perhaps, that around Kyoto a woman often seems to choose her husband on the basis of the man's mother as much as of the man himself. It's the mother-in-law who's going to be everywhere in the house, even as the husband may be seldom seen.

•

"The woman obeys the man," Confucius laid down in his *Book of Rites*. "In her youth she obeys her father and elder brother; when married, she obeys her husband; when her husband dies, she obeys her son."

•

"In today's world," a Chinese "mistress dispeller" told *The New Yorker* in 2017, "a secondhand woman is like a secondhand car. Once it's been driven, it's not worth a fraction of its original selling price." And a secondhand man? He has the lure, she says, of renovated real estate. "The value only appreciates."

●

Yet today far more women are visible in Chinese boardrooms than in Japanese. Japan has taken the Confucian model and, as in so many other respects, pushed it to its farthest extreme.

●

Boys in her world were allowed to sleep outstretched, an early-twentieth-century "samurai daughter" reported; but samurai girls had to adopt a stance while sleeping that represented *kinoji,* or the "spirit of control."

●

Thus women in Japan have every reason to make contact with a foreign world—by going abroad, by learning another language, even by marrying a foreigner—and men in Japan have every incentive to remain in a system that flatters and protects them.

•

After I got strip-searched every time I returned to Japan, a fellow traveler with equally dark skin told me how to avoid this: always go to the customs lane manned, so to speak, by a woman.

•

In response to all the opportunities denied them in the public sphere, Japanese women have traditionally made the most of the private.

•

In two out of every three Japanese households, it's the woman who handles all the earnings, giving her husband an average of 15 percent of his salary as pocket money.

•

In the night world—as at my local ping-pong club—women call the shots, precisely by pretending to allow men to assume they're in control.

A woman in Japan, James Merrill observed, "has less face to lose and proportionately more 'personality' than her refined husband."

•

Or, as Wilde's Mrs. Allonby has it, women "have a much better time" than men in this world. "There are far more things forbidden to us."

•

I used to think that Hello Kitty, the cartoon character who's cute, infantile and pretty in pink, was a model of how women are encouraged to be in Japan. Then I saw that being mouthless, as Hello Kitty is, is not the same as being toothless.

•

In 1965, four in every thousand Japanese marriages failed; forty years on, sixty did.

THE FAMILY WRIT LARGE

J apan is a society based more on trust than on faith; and lack of transparency can be less the enemy of trust than its perfect safeguard.

•

Couples on dates in Japan often prefer to sit side-by-side rather than face-to-face.

•

If a neighborhood is much like a family, addresses are relatively unimportant. Crime makes no more sense than robbing Peter to pay Paul. And people keep giving expensive presents to one another because they know that all the money is simply circulating within the same closed system.

•

My cosmopolitan, fashionable wife startles friends everywhere from Colorado to Tibet by reflexively referring to them as "Little Sister." They don't know that Japan is still enough of a traditional society that people address strangers as "Grandpa," "Father" or "Older Sister."

Ninety percent of Japanese women have defined themselves as "middle-class." More than half the country's citizens support just one of the country's twelve professional baseball teams, the Tokyo Giants. On New Year's Eve, nine in every ten television-owning households in Japan have at times been said to tune in to the same show, pitting a group of female singers against a group of men. But still the country around me remains a society based on a vertical, not a horizontal, model.

●

After Japan drew up a Victorian-style constitution in 1889, roughly one in every eighty citizens was qualified to vote. As the twentieth century began, every Japanese house-holder was still obliged to nail a wooden sign above his door on which was inscribed his name and his standing in society.

●

"A man of the lower class," wrote Basil Hall Chamberlain, at the turn of the twentieth century, "will often hold a partially opened fan in front of his mouth when addressing a superior, so as to obviate the possibility of his breath defiling the superior's face."

•

No choir can function without a conductor.

•

In North Korea, I'm regularly startled to encounter a Hermit Kingdom where a leader is taken to be a god, everyone marches to the beat of a single drummer and mass chants and calisthenics are daily enforced to remind everyone of collective responsibility. My neighbors in what for more than two centuries was itself a Hermit Kingdom tend not to think of most of this as strange—when they were young, they saw Japanese policemen arrest citizens for going to the movies, drinking coffee or eating sweet potatoes in the street. It's not North Korea's unbending upholding of order that unsettles my friends in Japan; it's their neighbor's indifference to boundaries.

•

One thief in Japan, after taking what he wanted, "would stay for a while," the scholar of Japanese literature Edward Seidensticker writes, "and talk with his victims, pointing out to them the advantages of watchdogs and well-locked doors."

•

This reverses the celebrated story of how, upon finding a thief in her hut, the nineteenth-century nun Rengetsu is said to have turned on the light, so he could do his job more effectively, then prepared tea and rice for the intruder.

•

The ratio of engineers to lawyers in Japan—of people building things as opposed to people organizing arguments—was forty-one times greater than in the United States for years after I arrived in Japan.

•

Free agency didn't exist in Japanese baseball till the 1990s. When, through a contractual loophole, the Osaka pitcher Hideo Nomo became the first Japanese to become a longtime player in the American major leagues, his father is believed to have stopped speaking to him.

•

In terms of wealth distribution, Japan in 2017 was "the most equal" society on the planet; many CEOs in Japan earn less than some of their employees do. But in terms of the gulf in public status, Japan is much more unequal than the United States. There's no overturning the hierarchy.

●

Japanese macaques are of interest to scientists, because, as one scientist says, they "are very status-conscious individuals. They're very intimidated by power." They will challenge only those lower in the pecking order. But they'll generally do this only in the company of the powerful.

●

My Japanese friends are as rattled by the idea of adoption as I would be if someone were to choose a child from a Humane Society shelter. Yet, traditionally, the Japanese thought nothing of taking on an orphaned nephew, a cousin studying far from home, even a prize pupil, as an adopted child. So long as he's within the circle, boundaries can be extended.

●

"The Japanese managed to create a competitive society *sans* competition," Arthur Koestler concluded in 1959.

•

The shock of the 2018 Japanese movie *Shoplifters* is that it shows a post-nuclear family so shattered that parents choose their children, children their parents. The deeper shock is that in this upside-down world—the photographic negative of the Japanese Dream—a tangle of lies somehow adds up to a truth and a family of criminals proves closer and more loving than one bound by blood.

•

An American instructor was upbraided, Joseph Campbell heard in Kyoto, for flunking a class of young women who had written papers that were word-for-word the same. A Japanese professor, Campbell was told at the same dinner, offered quite openly that he had taken his entire paper from another scholar.

•

All of them were diligently honoring tradition. The earliest historical texts in Japan, dating from 712 and

720 respectively, take whole incidents and speeches from Chinese history and present them as Japanese.

•

"Having to be different," noted the artist Robert Rauschenberg, famous for his enigmatic all-white canvases, "is the same trap as having to be the same."

THE OTHER SIDE OF SORROW

W e are taught that suffering is the one promise life always keeps," a Buddhist from Burma explains to a visiting American in the movie *Beyond Rangoon*. "So that if happiness comes we know it is a precious gift, which is ours only for a brief time."

•

After 9/11, many foreign observers were shocked that the terrorists' long-term strategy had reaped such dividends, leaving Americans traumatized for years; after 3/11—the "triple threat" of earthquake, tsunami and nuclear meltdown that took more than eighteen thousand lives in Japan in March 2011—foreign observers were shocked at how orderly and calm the Japanese remained, as if loss, and not its absence, is the norm. In Buddhism, the opposite of pleasure is not pain but delusion.

•

Mexico is happier, deep down, than the United States, my Mexican American friend Richard Rodriguez keeps telling me, because it has a tragic sense.

•

"Recent academic work," writes Andrew Solomon in *Far from the Tree,* "suggests that people who know their condition to be irreversible are happier than those who believe their condition may be ameliorated."

●

"You can alter behavior," says a woman in the Yasujiro Ozu film *The End of Summer,* "but you cannot alter character." In simpler cultures, behavior is taken to be a reflection of character.

●

Happiness thus becomes less the place where pain subsides than the one where the expectation of pleasure gets real.

●

If you constantly adapt to circumstances, however, will you ever be able to change them?

●

Twenty years before Camus was invoking Sisyphus as an emblem of futility, the Japanese philosopher Shuzo Kuki was affirming Sisyphus as a resident of Heaven, Christopher Benfey explains. The Japanese

Sisyphus, pushing a rock fruitlessly up a hill, "finds in this very repetition an entire system of morals and, consequently, all its happiness."

•

The Happiness Paradox states that happiness increases in relation to income until a certain point, after which income becomes immaterial.

The great exception is Japan. Incomes have gone up six times, adjusting for inflation, since the 1950s, yet people confess themselves less happy than before.

•

Is this because they are shy about claiming happiness? Wary of asserting it when everything could change? Or are they truly in despair?

•

"Emotions," writes the Zen philosopher D. T. Suzuki, "are just the play of light and shadow on the surface of the sea."

•

Which doesn't mean we don't feel them, only that we're unwise to take them to be something they are not.

OUT THE WINDOW

THE FARAWAY ISLAND

The only people in the world today who don't learn from Japan," Isamu Noguchi told his friend Saburo Hasegawa in Kyoto, soon after the war, "are the Japanese."

•

In Sei Shonagon's classic *Pillow Book,* from the early eleventh century, not a single foreigner is mentioned in all its two hundred and fifty-six pages. In the epic *Tale of Genji,* from the same insular Kyoto court, the only foreigners alluded to are some Korean astrologers in the opening chapter.

•

Foreign travel at the time was reserved for monks and priests who could bring back treasures from abroad.

•

In Victorian times, while the Grand Tour was flourishing, a Japanese man could be executed for trying to leave Japan, and a foreign vessel landing in Japan would be destroyed, and all its cargo and passengers slaughtered.

"To be told he is not a true Japanese," wrote my cousin's great-grandfather, visiting Japan in the 1930s, "was a greater punishment to a person than to be abused or even beaten."

●

"People here must be trying really hard not to learn English," a young visitor from New York said as we sat in a little Italian restaurant along the lantern-lit old lane of Pontocho, in a geisha district in Kyoto. "Because, whatever they set out to do, they do so well."

●

On English as a Foreign Language tests, the Japanese score lower in English proficiency than the North Koreans (and, as a two-time visitor to North Korea, I have not found English to be of Shakespearean levels in Pyongyang).

●

"In a foreign country, everything is a source of fear," wrote the boldest and most English-fluent of all modern Japanese novelists, Yukio Mishima, about living in New York. "You cannot go to the post office or to the bank, as you are frightened of going by yourself." The Japanese writer most celebrated for his time abroad, Natsume Soseki, did not entrust himself to a train or a cab in London: "their cobweb system is so complicated."

•

In the Commitment to Development Index's 2017 ranking of twenty-seven of the world's richest nations in terms of policies that benefit underdeveloped countries, Japan came second to last (ahead only of South Korea).

•

That same year, this country of one hundred and twenty-seven million accepted exactly twenty asylum-seekers, out of almost twenty thousand who were considered. In Canada and Germany, the rate of acceptance was 40,000 percent higher; a single Turkish town had taken in more than a hundred thousand refugees from Syria alone.

•

Japan is so good at functioning on its own terms that its people find it ever more challenging to function on the terms of the rest of the world.

Indeed, it's precisely the things that keep Japan out of step with the larger global community— its treatment of women, of outsiders, of those of different sexual orientation—that allow it to function so harmoniously with itself.

⁕

"Increasingly, she found it difficult to be off-campus anyway," writes Dave Eggers of a new employee at a spotless, state-of-the-art computer headquarters in Silicon Valley, in his 2014 novel, *The Circle*. "There were homeless people, and there were the attendant and assaulting smells, and there were machines that didn't work, and floors and seats that had not been cleaned, and there was, everywhere, the chaos of an orderless world."

⁕

The computer company Apple Inc. has sometimes seemed to be almost Japanese, not just because of its sleekly minimalist designs, or because of Steve Jobs's delight in the walled gardens of Kyoto, to which he took each of his children; but simply because it has maintained its perfection by operating within a tightly controlled closed system. It remakes the world by keeping most of the world out.

•

"Many of the qualities about the Danish system that work so well for those born into it have made it particularly hard for outsiders to penetrate," wrote Hugh Eakin in 2016, explaining why the friendly, prosperous, benign society of Denmark is often not so kind to refugees.

•

"To be completely Japanese," said Isamu Noguchi, who saw a lot by being incompletely Japanese, "you can not have a world viewpoint."

•

Japan is never going to flourish at the global game, says my savviest financier friend, who's made billions off his intuitions; its only hope in the twenty-first century is to market its otherness, its foreignness, and sell itself as a tourist destination. Precisely what makes it so frustrating to foreigners trying to do business there makes it fascinating to foreigners wishing to explore a deeply foreign culture.

•

At my smallish neighborhood train station in Nara, I'm greeted every day by a McDonald's outlet, a Kentucky Fried Chicken parlor, a Mister Donut store and a Starbucks café. The whole complex bears the title "Le Ciel," and across the street is a department store called "Paradis."

But when I step into McDonald's, it's to find Vegetable Juice on the menu. I can choose between Rosehip-and-Hibiscus Tea and Corn Potage Soup to go with my Petit Pancakes. Colonel Sanders across the way is sporting a kimono, as befits one who is doling out Wa-Tu Chicken cuttleballs, Tokumori Fish Cakes and Chinese Cabbage and Bacon au gratin.

At Starbucks, I'm invited to choose between Strawberry Mille-Feuille Crepes and Marshmallow and Nut Chocolate Cake; at Mister Donut, there's Shrimp Gratin Pie on sale and a poster for an "Ice cream au lait debut" under the ads for a Misdo Club Card (for frequent doughnut-eaters) and a sign defining the space as "San Francisco Chinatown." Even the other eateries in the station building—an Italian restaurant offering what it calls "Japolitan" cuisine, a "Thé Thé" tea room, next to the Nuku-Nuku eatery—don't fit into any lexicon I recognize.

In Japan, I'm reminded, nothing seems so foreign as the things I associate with home.

I was four when my parents divorced," says my old friend from Nagasaki. We've known each other for more than twenty years now, after meeting in a foreigners' café in his hometown. Whenever he comes to Nara, he mentions how "local" the place is, how he loves the quality of mystery around it. "You can still feel a real connection between the temples and the community, like in classical Japan. Even the weather is different in places around here like Asuka and Horyuji, the way the sun rises and sets."

Around us are pagodas and temples going back to the eighth century, when this was the capital of the land. Downtown is ruled by twelve hundred wild deer, who walk calmly along busy streets and halt traffic on the rare occasions when my four-legged neighbors refuse to wait for a green light.

"In those days," my friend goes on—speaking of 1964—"almost *no one* in Japan got divorced. Everyone in the neighborhood knew." His mother had gotten pregnant by another man, and left the house, abandoning four-year-old Joji, as I'll call him, in the care of a bewildered father who, three years later, married a second woman, who proved keener to lavish affection on her own two children than on the lost little boy she'd taken on.

"Then the man my mother went to join died. Cancer. And she married another man, and had another child."

The result—unusual for Japan, but hardly unknown—was that Joji had almost no contact with mother or stepmother or father or half-sibling or step-siblings; for as long as I've known him, he's been traveling—Myanmar, Iran, Maine, Australia, Nepal, Thailand, Afghanistan—and yet, like many a traveler, finding no home anywhere, even as he comes to see that the only home he has is the one that he is fleeing.

I think of the CDs lined up along every shelf in his little room, the gifts he keeps showering on me—T-shirts for ping-pong, apples from the north, even knickknacks for Hiroko, whom he's met just once.

"I saw my mother last week," he says, as we pass the stately four-story structure that is the second-highest pagoda in the land. It's no surprise she's on his mind.

"In Nagasaki?"

"Yes. It's difficult, because she knows I cannot love her. But she's ill."

Cancer again, epidemic in post-atomic Nagasaki. "It's not so bad," he says. "The government pays all her medical expenses. Because she was a victim of the A-bomb."

He pauses, and we walk around the little pond where a young lover of an ancient emperor plunged to her death.

"My father, too. It's not so bad. He was seven at the

time; she was five. He was in a park; she was in school. But afterwards they went to the center of the explosion, and caught the radiation. They didn't know."

In 1995, half a century after the atom bomb was dropped, a study found rates of leukemia among survivors in Nagasaki to be ten times higher than would otherwise be expected.

Yet Joji loves Dylan and jazz and the blues, and every last piece of America he can get; that was how we first met, he riffing wildly about *Saturday Night Live* and cheeseburgers as we reeled around the streets of Nagasaki late at night. He follows American affairs more closely than I do, has visited forty-six of the fifty states and is definitive on both Thanksgiving and the vagaries of American foreign policy.

"In Japan," Joji continues, "people don't know the world. They know even less than Americans do. They're not like the English, the Germans, the Australians. But also they don't know what to love about their own country. They have no direction. Only exam-knowledge, no real intelligence."

I'm used to this complaint from him, and it doesn't subside as he approaches his fiftieth birthday, eight days before the sixty-fifth anniversary of the dropping of the bomb on Nagasaki. It's the complaint of the no-longer-youthful almost everywhere, I think.

A young friend of Joji's strolls up—polite and quiet, engaging with his shy English, as he walks through the arcade—and when he strolls off across the Deer Park to fetch his car, I say to my old friend, "He seems nice. Innocent."

"Maybe. But so much counseling. Every night I have to counsel him, two, three hours. He has problems with his father."

"His father is unkind?"

"No. His father is a kind man. But he doesn't know what his son wants."

It's simple, as Joji sees it. Japan has left old Japan behind, and not found anything to replace it with. It can't be modern America, and it can't be ancestral Nihon.

As his friend pulls up, Joji wishes me a brisk, rather American goodbye—a jolly handshake—and I say, "Joji," when he gets into the car, wondering how much of what he's said about Japan may be a reflection of himself. "What is the best thing about Japanese culture?"

"Silence," he says, as he closes the door, and rolls down the window. "It's a silent world."

LEARNING TO BE FOREIGN

On an ever-more-global planet, Japan can look like a seventy-year-old man who dons a brand-new "I ♥ NY" T-shirt, but remains no less old for his youthful gear, and no less himself.

•

A foreigner sees contradiction in this, while a Japanese sees only compartments. Dessert, appetizers and the main course are often served in the same tray in a traditional Japanese restaurant.

•

Within a month of the end of World War II, the leading historian of the Occupation, John Dower, points out, around four hundred Japanese companies were manufacturing chewing gum. No one, however, was likely to mistake Osaka for Chicago.

•

Some foreigners, confronted by a place that looks and acts so different, try to become Japanese. They soon find that, the more they speak Japanese, the more they should pretend not to (nobody likes a trespasser); the more they want to be taken for themselves, the more they're seen as symbols of the outside world. Others go in the opposite direction, choosing to play bulls in a china shop, hyper-Falstaffs, like the Americans hired for pro-wrestling bouts in Japan in the 1950s who were paid handsomely to cheat and kick, thus confirming every stereotype of barbarians at the gates.

●

Japan does not permit dual nationality.

●

When I arrived in Japan, I noticed—and wrote about—how the word for "wrong" was the same as the word for "different." In truth, of course, it was I who had gotten it wrong, failing to understand the explanation a book had laid out. In effect, I was calling the Japanese wrong simply because they seemed so different.

●

"What do you do," I saw a Canadian in a large auditorium in Japan ask the Dalai Lama, after a talk, "if you really love a foreign culture and you really want to be part of it and you dream of being there for life, but everyone reminds you that you're different?" The leader of the Tibetans looked at the young man with a grandfather's warmth and said, "Frankly, I think you should go back to Canada."

•

Put another way, anyone who bows while speaking on the phone may have spent too long in Japan. Anyone who laughs at those bowing while speaking on the phone hasn't spent enough time here.

•

An American friend of mine in a Japanese organization in California took pains to make public acknowledgment of a sex scandal that had torn the group apart. Instantly he was berated by his American colleagues for giving the matter short shrift—and berated by his Japanese colleagues for mentioning it at all.

•

"I was no more than the Foreigner," observes an American narrator living in the Netherlands, in the Richard Powers novel *Galatea 2.2*, "but even that bit part wound me tighter into the social web than I'd ever been in my country."

On arrival in Japan, I recited all the standard guidebook proverbs—"The nail that sticks out must be hammered down." After I'd been here a while, the only proverb that seemed to make sense was the Buddhist maxim "Even the reverse has a reverse."

•

Every time I stressed how different Japan was from everywhere else, I found a near-perfect explanation of Japan—in a passage describing somewhere else.

•

"Our ancestors lacked the word 'individualism,'" Tocqueville wrote, "which we have created for our own use, because in their era there were, in fact, no individuals who did not belong to a group and who could consider themselves absolutely alone."

•

"It is sometimes said," writes Diana Eck, scholar of Hinduism, "that in India the 'individual' as we think of it in the West does not exist. A person thinks of himself or herself not as a singular entity, but rather as part of a larger interdependent whole, in which the parts mirror one another in an infinite, intricate pattern."

•

"Historically," the psychoanalyst Sudhir Kakar tells the Indian American writer Anand Giridharadas, "the fulcrum of the Indian family has been the parents-sons unit rather than the couple. . . . The couple is now taking center stage and is under great pressure, not only from the normal expectations that the partner fulfill all emotional needs, but also from the persistence of the former ideology, which leads to conflicts of loyalty, especially in a man who is torn between his wife on the one hand and his parents and siblings on the other."

•

"A man who knows the court," the seventeenth-century moralist La Bruyère wrote, "is a master of his gestures, of his eyes and of his face. . . . He is profound; impenetrable; he dissimulates bad offices, smiles at his enemies, controls his irritation, disguises his passion, belies his heart, speaks and acts against his feeling."

•

"We are very like bricks in a wall," writes Baden-Powell, in the "Citizenship" chapter of *Scouting for Boys*, "we each have our place, though it may seem a small one in so big a wall. But if one brick gets rotten, or slips out of place, it begins to throw an undue strain on others, cracks appear, and the wall totters."

•

"Just because we were lying," writes the Turkish novelist Orhan Pamuk, evoking the beloved Istanbul of his youth in *A Strangeness in My Mind,* "it didn't mean we weren't sincere. We understood one another's private motivations, while making sure to keep up public appearances."

•

"Wherever you find yourself, and in whatever circumstances," wrote Epictetus, "give an impeccable performance."

•

"Be suspicious," Epictetus also wrote, "if you appear to others as special."

Meeting the woman now my wife, I was struck by how much she'd grown up in Japan on the same global culture that had formed me, during the very same years, in England—*The Beverly Hillbillies,* Yogi Bear, "The Sound of Silence," cotton candy and Audrey Hepburn. Getting to know her a little, I ran into assumptions and responses I'd seldom meet in the West, as recorded throughout this book. Now that we've been together for more than thirty years, I find her—of course—little different in her anxieties and pleasures and jealousies from anyone I would meet anywhere.

Though always individual, in the same breath.

●

"FREE OF PEANUTS," it says in English on the front of my little bag of Kameda Seika rice crackers. On the back it says, "This product may contain traces of peanuts."

PLAYING BALL

The first year I visited Japan, two coaches from my local Hanshin Tigers baseball team beat up an umpire so violently that they were suspended for the rest of the season.

•

Two years later, an umpire at the Tigers' venerable ninety-five-year-old stadium, Koshien, had to be carried off the field after being hit by a bicycle chain flung by a fan.

•

In a country by every measure at least six times safer than the United States, an umpire from the States was prevented from working games in Japan, writes the leading American expert on Japanese baseball, Robert Whiting, on the grounds that it "was not safe to umpire in Japan."

•

You go to a baseball game in Japan, as to every other public event in Japan, not for the game—which is often cautious and flawless to a fault—but for the fans. The most exciting action is nearly always to be found in the stands.

●

In the neighborhood where I've lived for twenty-seven years, little girls hide behind their mothers' skirts every time they see me, dogs bare their teeth at me as I walk past, day after day for decades. At the ballpark, a grandmother I've never met beams down and offers me some of her fried octopus, and a huge stranger dressed from head to toe as a tiger wraps me in a bear hug.

●

Even a foreigner can become part of the team in a place where private passions are given vent in public and the slogan in the souvenir shop says (in English), LET YOUR YOU OUT.

●

When I took my wife to a professional baseball game in Los Angeles, she could hardly believe that fans were strolling around the grounds, heading off at critical moments to get jumbo helmets filled with nachos and leaving early to beat the traffic. In Japan you come to the park to cheer your team to victory.

After the Tigers finished last, the year I came to live in Japan—they were thirty-seven and a half games out of first place—the demand for tickets was so intense that, as Whiting writes, "even the benches in the outfield were converted into reserved seats, sold by lottery months in advance."

•

The full-time cheerleader choreographing the individual song and dance each one of us delivers for every player as he comes up to the Koshien plate has as many as thirty assistants; some such cheerleaders have been known to take attendance to make sure not a single assistant is missing.

•

Though the fans all around me are desperate for victory, the players are mostly trying not to lose. The first time an American, Bobby Valentine, was brought over to manage a professional Japanese team, in 1995, he was fired after leading his hapless squad to a stunning second-place finish, because, a team spokesman announced, "of his emphasis on winning."

In Japan, it pays to try not to lose (rather than to win), because a game ends in a tie if the score is level after four hours and twelve innings. In each of my first two years in Japan, the team with the most victories in the Pacific League, one of the country's two professional divisions, failed to claim the pennant because a team with fewer victories had more ties—and thus enjoyed a higher winning percentage.

•

My Tigers set a record for most home runs in a season in 1985. But they set a record that same season for most sacrifice bunts. Japanese players sacrifice up to three times more often than their American counterparts, a reminder that caution is enjoined even for the most powerful.

•

In the Japan Series, the country's modestly titled answer to the World Series, a Fighting Spirit Award is given each year to the most valuable player on the losing squad.

"Americans take their strength in victories," writes Don Winslow in *The Cartel,* his epic novel about *narcotraficantes.* "Mexicans' strength is in their ability to suffer loss."

•

Old World cultures cherish grace in defeat because they know we all lose in the end; New World cultures remain confident they can keep destiny at bay, perhaps forever.

•

In any case, winning is seen in a larger context in Japan. Sometimes foreign players will get walked with the bases loaded (so some cherished record can remain in Japanese hands).

•

Every August, TV stations across the country—including the government-run Educational Channel—broadcast the high-school baseball championships from Koshien from breakfast time till after dark, day after day for fifteen days. The ground on which the young emblems of purity enact their rites is so sacred that, as with certain temples, no woman is allowed to set foot on it.

•

There are no names on the white uniforms of the players on the forty-nine teams, and the teenagers are generally as shaven-headed as monks. When they're awarded walks, they sprint to first base.

•

From the age of nine, Ichiro Suzuki admitted—he had been taken by his father to a batting cage every day, for four hours, from the age of seven—he had "five to six hours [in a year] to play with friends."

•

In the New World, players are taken out of a game after throwing a hundred pitches; in Japan, pitchers in spring training have been known to throw four hundred and two pitches in a day, leading to brilliant careers that die as quickly as cherry blossoms.

•

When I arrived in Japan, the country was importing its stars from the Americas; now it exports its stars and more often imports its managers. The ability to lead is harder to find in the land of hesitation than the ability to follow.

●

A runner steals second base in a game his team is leading by twelve to two.

"Shameless!" I cry. "In America, that would be regarded as bush-league: to humiliate a team that is already having its face rubbed in the dirt."

"Is it better to go easy on them, treating them as kids?" asks my wife. "Isn't that a worse kind of humiliation?"

●

In a game between a Japanese squad and some visiting American all-stars, in November 2014, I watch the Japanese starting pitcher throw a perfect game for five innings, and then get taken out.

Is this so he won't humiliate the guests? To give others a chance to share in the glory? Because he'd been allocated only five innings?

I can only conclude that Yogi Berra was right: "If the world were perfect, it wouldn't be."

In the final game of the Japan Series, with the entire seven-month season on the line, suddenly, in the middle of the ninth inning, as one hundred and forty-six games come to their five-minute climax, the screen fills with ads for detergent. Another program is scheduled to begin at 9:00 p.m., and the prearranged schedule takes precedence over even the most exciting moment of the year.

ON THE HORIZON

The ghosts in Japan speak only Japanese, I'm tempted to believe; I've never been visited by one. Often I'll walk impervious through a Japanese grave-yard at dead of night while my wife cowers at the mere thought of it. Yet the presence of the past, a constant awareness of tradition and superstition, the influence of forefathers, can overwhelm me here, much more than in the Old World places where I grew up.

There we had ritual and precedents more than the specific wisdom of ancestors; we were surrounded by images and mementos of the dead, rather than of those who could be regarded as still living. But in Japan, death is not so much the opposite of life as its adjoining chamber, in a house of sliding panels. My neighbors make very strict distinctions between work and play, man and woman, foreigner and local, as if to tame a world in which the most essential things seldom honor hard-and-fast distinctions. The past is never behind us, and it's not easy to say where this moment ends and the time of the ancestors begins.

One cold winter night, I was standing beside a bed in a hospital, three blocks from Kyoto's eighth-century pagoda, when the pulse reading on a monitor began to sink. From 53 and 62 down to 36, 34, 31. Up again to 73, 106, 81, but then down to 24, 21, 27. When, at last, the red numeral settled at "0," and all our ministrations failed to coax it back up to 51, 63, 117, the dead woman's loved ones didn't stop talking to her, smoothing her hair, saying thank you to her. The sweet young nurse on duty suggested she not ask a doctor to come in to pronounce the woman dead for thirty or forty minutes, so late-arriving family could continue to greet the woman as if she were still alive.

For the next two days, no one around seemed to think twice about congratulating the ninety-year-old corpse on her calm, staring with fond delight at her waxen face and rigor mortis and—as would continue more or less for decades—taking cans of her favorite beer to place by her coffin and putting out food for her at every meal. She was still among us, even if more silent than she had been.

"I've always been afraid of Japan," said a friend from England, brought over for two weeks by a husband who'd been stationed here during the Occupation and was guiding her everywhere with the Japanese he'd retained. "And now I see I was right to be. It's so *foreign*, so different from anywhere I've seen. I mean, I've been to China and India, and India was shocking, but I loved it. This is different."

We were sitting in a California café in central Nara, surrounded by wooden temples and orange lanterns leading to the most sacred shrine in the land outside of Ise. She was staying in an elegant inn near the biggest Buddha on the planet, and her husband moved among the shops and restaurants as easily as if he were at home. The four of us had often met like this in London. But none of that was consoling to her.

"Before I came here, a friend in England told me, 'Japan is the future.' And, yes, that's true of Tokyo. Tokyo *is* the future. But everything else in Japan is deep, deep past. The bullet train whizzes you along, the cell phones all but live for you, the toilet seats leap up and make noises and even clean themselves when they're not talking to you. But you have to wear a special set of slippers just to go to the toilet. It's all custom, even the way you open the door to go to the loo."

It's true. We start amidst the giddy, amusement-park surfaces here, but very quickly begin to fall down an ever-deepening well where no lights are visible.

"I'm sorry," she went on, "I know you love it. . . ."

"No," I said, "I know what you mean. In a way, you're explaining why I live here. It's a riddle, and a rich and dense and grave one, often. I can't begin to imagine I know the first thing about it. I can't tell you what will happen tomorrow. I don't know who Hiroko will be next month—what she'll love, where she'll be in the cycle of her life, what new forms of old tradition she'll expect me to understand. It keeps me on my toes, alert.

"I suppose, if one's job, one's life is trying to live with the things one can't understand, then Japan is the biggest prize. Because it's the ultimate challenge."

"Yes," she said, clearly relieved she'd be back in London a few days later. "I suppose I can see that."

As I walked home, through the barely lit park that sits at the heart of the old capital, a twelve-hundred-year-old pagoda outlined in the distance, the "whee"-ing deer among the trees, I thought how much this side of the country begins to take root inside the visitor who stays here for a while.

Lafcadio Hearn, after his initial infatuation with the prettiness and courtesies of Japan, began to give himself over to excavating ghost stories, the "goblin" presences he felt all around him and what he called, eerily, "the sacrificial past . . . within." In the wake of the tsunami in 2011, there was a rush on exorcisms as "hungry ghosts"—those abruptly taken from the earth without time to prepare for another world—were said to cluster around northern Japan, often speaking through the living, and unprepared priests were obliged to expel demons.

My old friend Bill Powers, from MIT's Media Lab, was conducting a seminar near Kyoto in 2017 when the conversation turned to artificial intelligence. One of the high-level Japanese executives present—from a celebrated international communications company—said that the great blessing of artificial intelligence would be that it might allow us to converse more easily with the dead.

"I'd never thought of it like that," Bill said to me next day.

"Which of us would? That cutting-edge technology

might be not so much about surging into the future as more freely accessing the wise ghosts of the past?"

Sometimes Japan seems more than ready to change itself on the surface precisely so that it will never have to change deep down.

PLUS ÇA CHANGE?

The new day is almost here," writes Haruki Murakami in *After Dark*, "but the old one is still dragging its heavy skirts. Just as ocean water and river water struggle against each other at a river mouth, the old time and the new time clash and blend. Takahashi is unable to tell for sure which side—which world—contains his center of gravity."

•

Japan in the postwar years—this is Murakami's setting, his lament—has a door that's permanently half open.

"Are you coming in or going out?" one might ask the entire culture.

To which the answer—in a land of American surfaces and non-American values—is a shrug.

•

At the end of his hugely popular novel from 1947, Osamu Dazai notes, "However much the waves on the surface of the sea may rage, the water at the bottom, far from experiencing a revolution, lies motionless, awake but feigning sleep."

America defines itself by its future tense as much as Japan does by its past: the Golden Age in Japan— even more than in other elderly cultures—is always behind us. Dazai's novel about the Land of the Rising Sun, preoccupied with twilight, is called *The Setting Sun*.

●

It's less that Japan is foreign than that it so often recalls the world that we knew centuries ago. And no one can be sure of whether that's the past or the present.

●

"The front part of the home of a successful Japanese businessman," Joseph Campbell was told on his way to Japan, "will be in the Western style. . . . But his living quarters will be Japanese and without furniture; and when he returns in the evening, he puts off his Western garb and dons Japanese."

●

Perhaps a society where ancestors are all but indistinguishable from gods is always going to be slow to change. When the twenty-first century began, there were thirty thousand fortune-tellers to be found along the streets of Japan.

●

So, too, a culture where gods are believed to live in the very soil, air and waves will not die quickly, since such forces are never quite so perishable as temple and church.

●

Besides, a culture used to playing a part can open up to the West in 1853, remake itself on a foreign model in 1945 and still be what it always was, a culture adept at taking things from abroad and making them its own.

●

The center of Tokyo, wrote Tanizaki, with precision, is "a medieval castle with mossy walls and banks along its moat, set off against the finest modern buildings."

Japan's unique contribution to the postmodern world, maintains the contemporary Japanese philosopher Takeshi Umehara, is to see that everything is eternal and ephemeral at the same time.

•

Japan's toilets are famous for their ability to measure your urine sugar, to offer air-conditioning, to produce music to cover up a tinkle, even to self-deodorize. But when I go to my gleaming, twenty-second-century local train station, it's to be confronted by a squat-style "Asian" toilet as primitive and foul-smelling as anything in rural Tibet.

•

After he returned from his time in England, Japan's most beloved novelist—his face once on every thousand-yen note—Soseki devoted his mornings to reading English literature, his afternoons to copying out Chinese poetry. A country that still mixes in every sentence Chinese characters with characters that are transliterations of foreign words can look very much like Oscar Wilde's Dorian Gray.

"I traveled around Japan these last three years," says
my friend the techno-visionary Kevin Kelly, "and
I never saw a single broken roof tile. Not one. On
the other hand, I didn't see much new construction.
Maintenance: that's what Japan does."

"Old Japan is dead and gone," Basil Hall Chamberlain
writes at the beginning of his compendious five-
hundred-and-sixty-six-page encyclopedia from
the turn of the twentieth century, *Things Japanese,*
compiled after decades in the land, "and Young Japan
reigns in its stead." Three sentences later, he adds,
"Nevertheless . . . it [is] abundantly clear to those
who have dived beneath the surface of the modern
Japanese upheaval that more of the past has been
retained than has been let go."

Sixty-four pages on, however—proving that he's
Japanese enough to contradict himself constantly as
well as British enough to keep making categorical
assertions—Chamberlain, an early professor
of Japanese at Tokyo University, writes of how

"illusory are the common European notions of 'the unchanging East.'"

●

It's common to say, as I have just done, that Japan has long been torn between China and America, as between distant past and future. But as China grows ever more American in its capitalist ways and skyscraper cities, and as America looks ever more to the East to ground itself, Japan ends up ever more confused, not sure whether it's looking at everything with two faces or with none.

●

Perhaps Japan has been losing its soul for so long that it has a lot of soul to lose? Or loss itself is an illusion?

●

A country based around the seasons knows, after all, that everything is changing at every moment—three thousand five hundred and seven new restaurants are said to have opened up in Tokyo alone in 2015—and that fact never changes at all.

●

"The contradictions the mind comes up against," writes Simone Weil, "these are the only realities."

●

A young colleague comes in to Hayao Miyazaki's space, as shown in a documentary about the filmmaker, delighted that what appears to be the director's final film, a huge and all-consuming project, is behind them at last. The master animator, in his seventies, smiles and says, "The end is a new beginning."

THE END, A NEW BEGINNING

Since Japan seems to be in constant motion, we assume that if it's not necessarily getting any better it must be getting worse. But maybe running in place is precisely how it keeps itself intact?

•

An identity may be no less strong for being an identity crisis as well.

•

The holiest shrine in the land, at Ise, is completely rebuilt every twenty years, and all the twenty-five hundred ceremonial objects and instruments within the shrine are carefully re-created. The wood for the new building comes from trees that are more than three hundred years old, the pillars from trees that have been standing for more than five hundred. Every twenty years, the shrine is made not new again, but old.

•

Or maybe Japan is changing, slowly, under the surface? As of 2016, barely 2 percent of Japan's population was foreign-born (as opposed to the more than 50 percent in Western cities such as London and Toronto). Yet the number of international marriages went up tenfold between 1965 and 2007, to the point where one in every ten weddings in Tokyo included a Japanese and a foreigner.

●

In 2016, Miss Japan was a part-Indian called Priyanka, much as the winner of the Miss Universe Japan contest the previous year had been part African American.

●

Two years later, it was partly Haitian-American Naomi Osaka, with her 119-mile-per-hour serves and unflappable poise, who demolished Serena Williams in the U.S. Open to claim Japan's first major tennis championship.

●

Such *"hafu"*s have been fashionable on TV for decades, but now, it seems, the phrase you see on Japanese vending machines—"Blend Is Beautiful"— is seeping more and more into the culture.

"The spirit of Tawaraya has not changed in three hundred years," Toshi Okazaki Satow, eleventh-generation owner of Kyoto's most celebrated traditional inn, told me of her place. "But the style has to change to keep that spirit alive."

Thus she included Indonesian and Chinese and Egyptian accents in a deeply Japanese setting, and introduced telephones and televisions, but covered in traditional fabrics.

"It's by bringing in new elements," she explained, "that we keep everything old."

"Tradition is not simply 'preservation,'" the director emeritus of Kyoto's National Museum of Modern Art was quoted as saying in *Kyoto Journal* in 2018. "It is that element in creative art which does not change at its core but which changes constantly in its expression."

Hokusai was said to have moved ninety-three times in his life and taken on thirty-one noms de plume. But for seventy years he kept on painting Fuji.

•

"The only thing I know about war are two things," Dwight D. Eisenhower announced at a press conference. "The most changeable factor in war is human nature in its day-to-day manifestation; but the only unchanging factor about war is human nature."

•

"Looking at things from a broad perspective," the wartime Showa emperor told a journalist in 1975, "I do not think there has been any change between prewar and postwar."

A LETTER FROM A FRIEND

One late-autumn morning, I receive a letter from an elegant Japanese painter whom I've met only twice, very briefly (the first time I was introduced to him, he gave me and Hiroko a dazzlingly elegant big abstract canvas—a richer and more mysterious Rothko, all impeccable stripes of red and black—as a wedding present, the only one we received, in fact, since we made no ceremony of our trip to City Hall).

Now, from the wild and windswept shaman's island near Tokyo to which my friend has decamped, in his late sixties, in flight perhaps from his samurai background (he spends time with members of the imperial family, and used to live with a Mitsubishi heiress), he writes me a letter of many short pages, the strong black strokes of his English-language calligraphy allowing, in the classical way, for just a couple of sentences on every sheet.

Last night we had a strong typhoon that passed over the island. So I took your book for the night under fearful wind; it was perfect.

After a few hours, I started thinking about my father. Our family just escaped from China right after the Second World War by the last refugee ship leaving Shanghai. I was about four years old, so I remember people packed in the bottom of the ship and an oily smell, and what kind of clothes I was wearing.

We came back to Nagasaki (my father's home) safely. But unfortunately the city was already completely wiped out by the A-bomb.

My first footstep in Japan I encountered American M.P. [Military Police]. They sprayed me with D.D.T. from top to bottom, so I became a white boy. We left Nagasaki soon and lived in Tokyo ever since.

But my father never took us back to Nagasaki again and did not ever talk about it till he died.

More than fifty years passed after the war, and I visited Nagasaki. I wandered around the city all day, looking for something that did not exist any more. At night I ended up at the harbor, standing alone in the rain blankly for a while with no umbrella.

Then, suddenly, I broke down crying, burst into tears. I was surprised but calmly I watched over floods of tears for some time. I do not know how long it lasted, but I was sure it was not myself, but my father crying. It was the first time I witnessed his hard emotional expression through me, twenty years after his death.

Thank you so much for your existence.

S. NOTOMI.

A NOTE ABOUT THE AUTHOR

Pico Iyer is the author of more than a dozen books, translated into twenty-three languages. His four recent TED Talks have received more than eight million views so far. In the summer of 2019, he was Ferris Professor of Journalism at Princeton, guest director of the Telluride Film Festival and the first official writer-in-residence at Raffles Hotel in Singapore.

A NOTE ON THE TYPE

This book was set in Minion, a typeface produced by the Adobe Corporation specifically for the Macintosh personal computer, and released in 1990. Designed by Robert Slimbach, Minion combines the classic characteristics of old-style faces with the full complement of weights required for modern typesetting.

TYPESET BY SCRIBE, PHILADELPHIA, PENNSYLVANIA

PRINTED AND BOUND BY LSC COMMUNICATIONS, CRAWFORDSVILLE, INDIANA

DESIGNED BY IRIS WEINSTEIN